Muayed Sattar Al-Huse...,

Optimal Realization of the Rijndael Algorithm on Xilinx Platforms

Muayed Sattar Al-Huseiny

Optimal Realization of the Rijndael Algorithm on Xilinx Platforms

LAP LAMBERT Academic Publishing

Impressum / Imprint
Bibliografische Information der Deutschen Nationalbibliothek: Die Deutsche Nationalbibliothek verzeichnet diese Publikation in der Deutschen Nationalbibliografie; detaillierte bibliografische Daten sind im Internet über http://dnb.d-nb.de abrufbar.
Alle in diesem Buch genannten Marken und Produktnamen unterliegen warenzeichen-, marken- oder patentrechtlichem Schutz bzw. sind Warenzeichen oder eingetragene Warenzeichen der jeweiligen Inhaber. Die Wiedergabe von Marken, Produktnamen, Gebrauchsnamen, Handelsnamen, Warenbezeichnungen u.s.w. in diesem Werk berechtigt auch ohne besondere Kennzeichnung nicht zu der Annahme, dass solche Namen im Sinne der Warenzeichen- und Markenschutzgesetzgebung als frei zu betrachten wären und daher von jedermann benutzt werden dürften.

Bibliographic information published by the Deutsche Nationalbibliothek: The Deutsche Nationalbibliothek lists this publication in the Deutsche Nationalbibliografie; detailed bibliographic data are available in the Internet at http://dnb.d-nb.de.
Any brand names and product names mentioned in this book are subject to trademark, brand or patent protection and are trademarks or registered trademarks of their respective holders. The use of brand names, product names, common names, trade names, product descriptions etc. even without a particular marking in this work is in no way to be construed to mean that such names may be regarded as unrestricted in respect of trademark and brand protection legislation and could thus be used by anyone.

Coverbild / Cover image: www.ingimage.com

Verlag / Publisher:
LAP LAMBERT Academic Publishing
ist ein Imprint der / is a trademark of
OmniScriptum GmbH & Co. KG
Heinrich-Böcking-Str. 6-8, 66121 Saarbrücken, Deutschland / Germany
Email: info@lap-publishing.com

Herstellung: siehe letzte Seite /
Printed at: see last page
ISBN: 978-3-659-37451-7

Dedication:

To my Imam;

To my Parents,

Brothers, Sisters, Soulmate

&

My Gorgeous Kids

With Love

In His Holy Name

"Allah Will Raise Those Who Have Believed Among You and Those Who Were Given Knowledge, By Degrees"

Surat Al-Mujadila-11

Contents

1

Introduction

1.1. Background:

O ver the centuries, an elaborate set of protocols and mechanisms have been created to deal with information security issues while conveying the information by physical means. Often, the objectives of information security cannot be solely achieved through mathematical algorithms and protocols alone, but require procedural techniques and abidance of laws to achieve the desired result.

The requirements of information security within an organization have undergone two major changes in the last several decades. Before the widespread use of data processing equipment, the security of information (deemed to be valuable to an organization) was provided primarily by physical and administrative means. An example of the former is the use of rugged filling cabinets with a combination lock to store sensitive documents. An example of the later is personnel screening procedures used during the hiding process [1].

With the introduction of the programmable machines (computer), the need for automated tools to protect files and other information stored on computer has become eminent. This is especially the case for a shared system, such as a time sharing system, and the need is even more acute for systems that can be accessed over public telephone or data network such as the internet. The generic name for the collection of tools designed to protect data and to thwart hackers is computer security [1][2].

The second major change that affects security is the introduction of distributed systems and the use of networks and communications facilities for carrying data between terminal user and computer and between computer and computer [1][2].

Cryptography which is the study of mathematical techniques related to aspects of information security such as confidentiality, data integrity, entity authentication, and data origin authentication, is not the only means of providing information security, but rather one set of techniques characterized by being systematic, realizable (mostly), and having got a lot of work done with respect to it [2][1].

Cryptography is in general, divided into two major classes, the public and the secret key methods, with the former being characterized by, having two keys, one for use by the others, to encrypt the data intended for the owner of the key (namely the public key), and the other key is only known, and used by the owner to decrypt the received data (namely the private key). The later method has only one key, and depends in secrecy on different approaches.

Secret key methods can be classified into two groups, namely block and stream ciphers. Block ciphers encrypt and decrypt in multiples of blocks, and stream ciphers encrypt and decrypt at arbitrary data sizes. Block ciphers are mostly based on the idea by Shannon, that sequential application of confusion and diffusion, will obscure redundancies in the plaintext (the information to be encrypted), where confusion involves substitutions to conceal redundancies, and statistical patterns in the plaintext. Diffusion on the other hand involves transformations (or permutations), to dissipate the redundancy of the plaintext, by spreading it out over the ciphertext (the information after encryption). DES (Data Encryption Standard) and Rijndael (Advanced Encryption Standard) are examples of algorithms based on this approach.

Since early time, cryptographists realized that in order to fulfill the systematic characteristic, machinery and automation must be taken into consideration. Accordingly, many cryptographic machines were introduced most famous of them is the Enigma. Until the involvement of computers and other digital systems, these machines were mechanical. After the appearance of computer based systems, the most striking point has proved to be the realization of the cryptographic procedure, that is to say the method by which the cryptographic algorithm is implemented. Two main approaches arose with this regard:

The software implementation, which has the features of ease of use, ease of upgrade, portability, and flexibility as advantages, but with only limited physical security, especially with respect to key storage.

The characteristics of modern cryptographic algorithms and standards, allow simple hardware implementations, or fast computer implementations by the use of simple arithmetic. However, they are not fast enough to encrypt, large volumes of data in real time; for example an ANSI C implementation of Rijndael, which is adopted as the Advanced Encryption Standard (AES) by US Government to replace the DES requires 950 processor cycles per block on the x86 architecture**[3][4].**

Conversely, cryptographic algorithms (and their associated keys) that are implemented in hardware are, by nature, more physically secure as they cannot be easily read or modified by an outside attacker. Besides, hardware implementations have the potential of running substantially faster than software implementations [5].

1.2. Other Implementations:

a. Amphion 2003 [6] delivered a commercial product for AES, with Xilinx virtex E-8 FPGA. It is a key agile implementation (encryption key is generated on-chip), with a single round (unrolled loop), with an unspecified pipelining. Its core uses a highly (as they claim) optimized HDL core. It must be said here that the implementation details are not reported by the authors. The design gives the following readings:-

1. Max clock: 91.5 MHz.
2. Max throughput: 1.061 Gbps.
3. Hardware used: 573 CLB slices.
4. H/W: 1.85 Mb/sec.slices TPS.
5. H/W: 10 block RAMs.

b. Chodowiec and Gaj 2003 [7] proposed a compact FPGA architecture for the AES algorithm, with 128 bits key, targeted for low-cost embedded applications. This is achieved by folding the iterative architecture to minimize the circuit area. First of all, they suggest changing the order of the operations proposed by the standard as follows: ShiftRow, SubByte, MixColumn, then AddRoundkey, resulting in consecutive SubByte and MixColumn, and hence, the algorithm operations can be thought of as 32 bits operations with four clocks per round rather than 128 bits operations with one clock per round. This will reduce the resources to only 25%. Such a configuration gives the following readings:-

1. Max clock: 60 MHz.
2. Max throughput: 166 Mbps.
3. Hardware used: 222 CLB slices.
4. H/W: 0.63 Mb/sec.slices TPS.
5. H/W: 3 block RAMs.

c. Elbirt *et al* 2002 [8] used several approaches to implement the five algorithms proposed to be the AES. Most successful approach for implementing the Rijndael involves a two-stage partial pipeline with a one sub-pipeline

3

optimized for speed. Their sub-pipeline is in fact a splitting of the partial pipeline stage into two sub-stages. Putting in mind that half of the delay within each stage is due to the S-box substitutions and separating it from the rest of the stage functions would balance the delay between the sub-pipeline stages. Consequently, sub-pipelining by dividing the S-boxes, would be a nontrivial task. Their work results are as follows:-

1. Max throughput: 0.95 Gbps.
2. Hardware used: 4871 CLB slices.
3. H/W: 0.1948 Mb/sec.slices TPS.

d. Kwon *et al* 2002 [9] employed basic (loop) architecture with full loop unrolling that is to say, all rounds are designed and tied in a line. Their design supports all three key lengths: 128,192, and 256. The authors do not give any details as to how they implement their platform specific design. While instead they concentrated on how to interface the Xilinx virtex xcv300pq240-4 chip to a PCI card with FPGA accelerator board. Their results are as follows:-

1. Max clock: 30 MHz.
2. Max throughput: 167 Mbps.
3. Hardware used: 2256 CLB slices.
4. H/W: 0.074 Mb/sec.slices TPS.

e. Siddeeq Ameen 2005 [10] made use of the AES to design security system as part of a client server network. The system uses in addition to the AES the message digest(MD5), data compression, data scrambling, traffic padding, novel PN sequence generator(that is based on the AES) and the RSA. The AES is software implemented by using C++ language.

f. Weavever and Wawrzynek 2004 [11] optimized their key agile AES implementation design for throughput utilizing a Virtex E-600-8 and a 128 bits key. The following are the parameters produced by the design:-

1. Max clock: 115MHz.
2. Max throughput: 1.75 Gbps.
3. Hardware used: 770 CLB slices.
4. H/W: 1.7 Mb/sec.slices TPS.
5. H/W: 10 block RAMs.

The design has a single round with internal pipelining (sub or intra round pipelining or C-slow retiming), thus, instead of placing a single register at the output, C separate registers are placed along the path from the input to the output. The authors suggest to start with latency optimized design and then add registers. This requires that every computation is properly aligned in the pipeline. The above description makes use of hand mapping approach in order to adjust the space timing for different pipeline stages. The most interesting point to be noticed about this design is the lack of systematic approach.

    g. Weawever and Wawrzynek 2004 [11] optimized their key agile AES implementation design, for latency, on SpartanII 100-5, with 128 bits key, getting:-

      1.   Max clock: 155 MHz.
      2.   Max throughput: 1.3 Gbps.
      3.   Hardware used: 770 CLB slices.
      4.   H/W: 2.3 Mb/sec.slices TPS.
      5.   H/W: 10 block RAMs.

The design employs a single round with no internal pipelines and with a single set of registers on the outputs. The inputs to the round are multiplexed among the input data and the previous round outputs with the agile sub-key generator constructed in the same manner. In addition to a single register between the output sub-keys and the core of the cipher.

To limit the critical path; the control logic is a simple counter and a small amount of logic, only one block can be encrypted at a time with cock cycles equal to the number of rounds in the cipher. This implementation, is straightforward and has a little of invention.

1.3. Aims of The Work:

a. To study the Rijndael algorithm with hardware implementation in mind. This includes reviewing the original and the reviewed documentations related to the AES regardless of the implementation issues as an initial step.

b. To review the most successful approaches of implementation of the Rijndael algorithm. This includes software, parallel processing units, and reconfigurable hardware approaches.

c. To investigate the points of significant effect on implementation by putting the internal structure of the host hardware in perspective while making decision about how to redo the algorithm.

d. To propose a design, and implementation on a chosen hardware platform and show its advantage over other implementations.

e. To draw comparisons with the other implementations by using the same criteria available from those implementations.

1.4. Book Layout:

The study is divided into six chapters and three appendices the content of which is briefed below:

Chapter one presents an introduction to security of information and the AES, it also includes a review of some of the implementations in the literature relevant to the aim of this study.

Chapter two deals with the concept of cryptography in general terms. It gives a step by step description of the AES with some reflection of the history of the algorithm. Finally, a worked example implemented with Matlab is provided.

Chapter three talks about the programmable devices and lists a group of the well-known devices ending with the most important of these, thats the Xilinx FPGAs. A detailed description of the internal architecture and rules for efficient use of these devices is also provided.

Chapter four presents the proposed design including the implementation of each of the AES operations on Xilinx® FPGA platforms.

Chapter five gives a worked example to compare the results of encrypting a plaintext by using VHDL code implementation simulated with ModelSim® and encrypting the same text by using the implementation of the AES on the Xilinx® FPGA. Also we make a comparison of the implementation parameters of our design with the parameters produced by the implementations of other authors.

In addition, there are three appendices at the end of this book which are as follow:

Appendix A describes the detailed encryption process for the example of Chapter 2.

Appendix B describes some necessary mathematical topics.

Appendix C details the Timing Reports for the implementation of the proposed design on the Xilinx VirtexII FPGA by using the ISE 4.1 software.

2

Techniques of Cryptography and the AES

2.1 Introduction:

Conventional encryption, also referred to as symmetric encryption or single-key encryption was the only type of encryption in use prior to the development of public key encryption. It remains by far the most widely used of the two types of encryption. One of the major issues with conventional systems is assumed that all parties know the set of encryption/decryption transformations (i.e., they all know the encryption scheme). The only information which should be required to be kept secret is the key.

There are two classes of conventional encryption schemes, which are commonly distinguished: *block ciphers* and *stream ciphers* [4]. *A stream cipher* is an encryption scheme which treats the plaintext as block of unity length. A *block cipher* on the other hand is an encryption scheme which breaks up the plaintext messages to be transmitted into strings called *blocks* (of a fixed length), and encrypts one block at a time.

In conventional encryption schemes, several operations are used to disguise the information contained in a message (plaintext). Examples of these operations include substitution and transposition. A substitution in a round is said to add *confusion* to the encryption process whereas a transposition is said to add *diffusion* [12].
Confusion is intended to make the relationship between the key and ciphertext as complex as possible. Diffusion refers to rearranging or spreading out the bits in the message so that any redundancy in the plaintext is spread out over the ciphertext.

Simple substitution and transposition ciphers do not (individually) provide very high level of security. However, by combining these transformations it is possible to obtain strong ciphers schemes. A round of encryption scheme then can be said to add both confusion and diffusion to the encryption. Most modern block cipher systems apply number of rounds in succession to encrypt plaintext.

2.2 Stream Ciphers:

Stream ciphers form an important class of symmetric-key encryption schemes. They are in one sense very simple block ciphers having block length equal to one. What makes this approach useful is the fact that the encryption transformations can change for each symbol of plaintext being encrypted.

In situations where transmission errors are highly probable stream ciphers are advantageous because they have no error propagation. They can also be used when the data must be processed one symbol at a time. For example when the equipment has no memory or buffering of data is limited. A stream cipher applies simple encryption transformations according to the key stream being used.

The key stream could be generated at random or by an algorithm that generates the key stream from an initial small key stream (also known as the *seed*). The key stream can otherwise be generated by using a dedicated algorithm from a seed and previous ciphertext symbols. Such an algorithm is called a *key stream generator*.

An example of stream cipher is the *Vernam Cipher*. This approach is defined on the alphabet $A = \{0, 1\}$. A binary message: $(m_1 m_2 \ldots m_t)$ is operated on by a binary key string: $(k_1 k_2 \ldots k_t)$ of the same length to produce a ciphertext string: $(c_1 c_2 \ldots c_t)$ where:

$$c_i = m_i \oplus k_i, \qquad 1 \leq i \leq t. \qquad \qquad \ldots\ldots(2.1)$$

If the key string is chosen randomly and used only once in the encryption session the Vernam cipher is then called a *one-time system* or a *one-time pad* [2]. The one-time pad can be shown to be theoretically unbreakable. That is, if a cryptanalyst has a ciphertext string: $(c_1 c_2 \ldots c_t)$ encrypted using a random key string which has been used only once, the cryptanalyst can do no better than guess that the plaintext being any binary string of length t. In other words all binary strings with t bits length are equally likely as plaintext [2][3].

It has been proven that to realize an unbreakable system requires a random key of the same length as the message. This limitation reduces the practicality of the system in all but few specialized situations. Reportedly, until very recently the

8

communication line between Moscow and Washington was secured by a one-time pad. Interestingly though, transport of the key was done by trusted courier [2].

2.3 Block Cipher and Standards:

Block ciphers differ from stream ciphers in that they encrypt and decrypt information in fixed size blocks rather than encrypting and decrypting each letter or word individually. A block cipher passes a block of data or plaintext through its algorithm to generate a block of ciphertext.

Ideally, a block cipher should generate ciphertext roughly equivalent in size (number of blocks) to the plaintext. A cipher that generates a block of ciphertext that is significantly larger than the information that a ciphering algorithm is trying to conceal is of little practical value [13].

For decades, the encryption standard in the United States has been the Data Encryption Standard (DES). However, the DES algorithm is no longer as secure as it once was and needed to be replaced. In 1999, NIST issued a new version of its DES standard (FIPS PUB 64-3) [15]. It was indicated that DES should only be used for legacy systems and that triple DES (3DES) can be used instead.

Triple DES has two attractions that assured its widespread use over the next few years. First, with its 168-bit key length it overcomes the vulnerability to brute-force attack of DES. Second, the underlying encryption algorithm in 3DES is the same as in DES. This later point means that legacy system can be upgraded with minimal cost and effort.

The principal drawback of 3DES is that the algorithm is relatively sluggish in software. The original DES was designed for mid 1970s hardware implementation and does not produce efficient software code. 3DES, which has three times as many rounds as DES is correspondingly slower.

A secondary drawback is that both DES and 3DES commonly use a 64-bit block size to produce ciphering efficient enough. For reasons of both efficiency and security a lager block size is desirable.

This move to upgrade DES and blow some life in it was a matter of buying time. The reality is that the underlying vulnerabilities in DES are directly passed to 3DES. As a result, in 1997 the NIST commissioned a competition to select a new algorithm to be used as the new standard for block cipher. This algorithm should have security strength, equal to or better than 3DES, and significantly improved efficiency. The new standard is called the Advanced Encryption Standard (AES). This standard is intended for use worldwide free of royalty fees [13] [15].

In addition to these general requirements, NIST specified that AES must be a symmetric bock cipher with a block length of 128 bits. The algorithm also has support for key lengths of 128, 192, and 256 bits.

In a first round of evaluation, 15 proposed algorithms were accepted. A second round narrowed the field to five algorithms. NIST completed its evaluation process and published a final standard (FIPS PUB 197) in November of 2001.

In the course of its evaluation this new algorithm has been subjected to more scrutiny than any other encryption algorithm over a longer period of time, and no effective cryptanalytic attack based on the algorithm other than the hypothetical brute force attack has been found to crack the algorithm.

Rijndael algorithm was selected as the new AES algorithm. Rijndael was designed to have the following characteristics [1]:-

a. Resistance against all known attacks.
b. Speed and code compactness on a wide range of platforms.
c. Design simplicity

2.4 AES Criteria:

The new AES to standards is supposed to have a number of features categorized in three groups, security, cost, and algorithm and implementation characteristics [1].

i. **Security,** which can be defined by the following:-

a. The actual security compared to other submitted algorithms (at the same key and block size).
b. The randomness, which is the extent to which the algorithm output is distinguishable from a random permutation on the input block.
c. The soundness of the mathematical basis for the algorithm's security.

ii. **Cost,** which can be defined by the following:-

a. The licensing requirements, where the specified AES is intended to be available on a worldwide, non-exclusive, and royalty-free basis.

b. The computational efficiency, where the evaluation will be applicable to hardware and software implementations. Computational efficiency essentially refers to the speed of the algorithm.

c. The memory requirements, such that the memory required implementing a candidate algorithm (for both hardware and software implementations of the algorithm) must also be considered. Memory requirements should include such factors as gate counts for hardware implementations, and code size and RAM requirements for software implementations.

iii. **Algorithm and Implementation Characteristics**, which can be defined by the following:-

a. The flexibility, where algorithms with greater flexibility will meet the needs of more users than less flexible ones. Flexibility may include the following:
   1. The algorithm can accommodate additional key and block sizes.
   2. The algorithm can be implemented securely and efficiently in a wide variety of platforms and applications.
   3. The algorithm can be implemented as a stream cipher, message authentication code (MAC) generator, pseudorandom number generator, hashing function, and etc.

b. The Hardware and software suitability such that the algorithm should not be restrictive in the sense that it can only be implemented in hardware. If one can also implement the algorithm efficiently in firmware then this would be an advantage in the field of flexibility.

c. The simplicity, where the algorithm must be judged according to relative simplicity of design.

2.5 Rijndael Algorithm:

The Rijndael algorithm defined a cipher in which the block length and the key length can be independently specified to be 128, 192, or 256 bits. A number of AES parameters which depends on the key length is given in Table (2.1). In the description in this study, a key length of 128 bit is assumed, which is likely to be, the one most commonly implemented [1].

Table (2.1): AES Parameters.

Key size(Nk word/bytes/bits)	4/16/128	6/24/192	8/32/256
Plaintext block size(Nb words/bytes/bits)	4/16/128	4/16/128	4/16/128
Number of rounds Nr	10	12	14
Round key size(words/bytes/bits)	4/16/128	4/16/128	4/16/128
Expanded key size(words/bytes)	44/176	52/208	60/240

Rijndael is a symmetric block encryption algorithm that encrypts blocks of 128, 192, or 256 bits and uses symmetric keys of 128, 192, or 256 bits, where all combinations of block and key lengths are possible. Each block of plaintext is encrypted several times with a repeating sequence of various functions in so-called rounds.

The number of rounds Nr depends on the block length Nb and key length Nk. If at least the block or key length is 256 bits, there are 14 rounds, if both the block and key length are 128 bits there are 10 rounds. In all other cases there are 12 rounds. Figure (2.1) shows the overall structure of Rijndael.

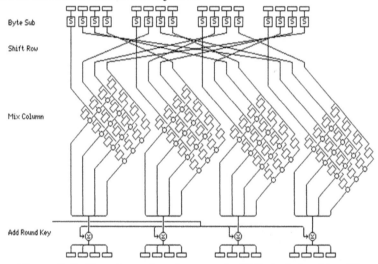

Figure (2.1): Transformations in a round of Rijndael algorithm [1]

The algorithm consists of an initial round *(AddRoundKey)* and Nr standard rounds. The first Nr-1 rounds are similar and they consist of four transformations, respectively: *ByteSub* (Substitution of bytes), *ShiftRow* (Shift rows), *MixColumn*

(Multiply columns) and *AddRoundKey* (XORing with key). The last round has only three of the transformations: *ByteSub, ShiftRow* and *AddRoundKey*.

At the start of the Cipher, the input is copied to an array called **State**. After an initial Round Key addition, the State array is transformed by implementing a round function 10, 12, or 14 times (depending on the key length). The as mentioned earlier final round is slightly differing from the first Nr-1 rounds.

The final State is then produced as the output. The round function is parameterized by a key schedule that consists of a one-dimensional array of four-byte words derived by using the Key expansion routine.

Several comments can be made regarding the structure of Rijndael:

1. The structure of the algorithm is not a Fiestel structure. In classical Fiestel structure half of the block is used to modify the other half of the data block and then the halves are swapped.

2. The key that is provided as input is expanded into an array of forty elements. Each element is formed of four 32-bit words, w[i]. Therefore, four distinct words (totaling 128 bits) serve as round key for each round.

3. The four stages at a standard round provide the required operations of permutation and substitution:-

   i. Substitute bytes: Uses an S-box to perform a byte by byte substitution of the block.

   ii. Shift rows: A simple permutation.

   iii. Mix columns: A substation that makes use of arithmetic over GF (2^8).

   iv. Add round key: A simple bitwise XOR of the current block with a portion of the expanded key.

4. The structure is quite simple. For both encryption and decryption the cipher begins with an Add Round Key stage followed by nine rounds. Each round includes all four stages. This is followed by the tenth round of three stages.

5. Only the Add Round Key stage makes use of the key. For this reason the cipher begins and ends with an Add Round Key stage. Any other stage applied at the beginning or end is reversible without knowledge of the key and so would add no security.

6. The Add Round Key stage is in effect, a form of Vernam cipher which alone would not be formidable. The other three stages together provide confusion, diffusion, and nonlinearity. By themselves those stages would not enough security

because they do not use the key. The cipher can be viewed as alternating operations of XOR encryption (Add Round Key) followed by scrambling of the block (the other three stages) followed by XOR encryption, and so on. This scheme is both efficient and highly secure.

7.   Each stage is easily reversible. For the ByteSub, ShiftRow and MixColumn stages, an inverse function is used in the decryption algorithm. For the AddRoundKey stage the inverse is achieved by XORing the same round key to the block by using the fact that A ⊕ A ⊕ B = B.

8.   As with most block ciphers the decryption algorithm makes use of the expanded key in reverse order. However, the decryption algorithm is not identical to the encryption algorithm. This is a consequence of the particular structure of AES.

9.   The final round of both encryption and decryption consists of only three stages. Again, this is a consequence of the particular structure of AES and is required to make the cipher reversible

2.5.1   The State:

The operations of AES algorithm are performed on a two-dimensional array of bytes called State. The state consists of four rows of bytes. Each row contains **Nb** bytes, where **Nb** is the block length divided by 32. In the state array denoted by the symbol s, each individual byte has two indices with its row number r in the range $0 \leq r < 4$ and its column number c in the range $0 \leq c < 4$. This allows an individual byte of the State to be referred to as either $s_{r,c}$ or $s[r,c]$. For the AES, **Nb**=4, i.e., $0 \leq c < 4$.

At the start of the Cipher and Inverse Cipher, the input array which is an array of bytes (in_0, in_1,....in_{15}) is copied into the state array as illustrated in Figure (2-2).

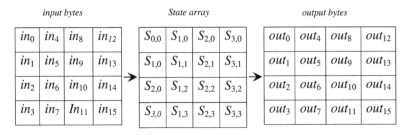

Figure (2-2): State array formation.

The cipher or Inverse Cipher operations are then conducted on the State array. After that the resulting bytes are copied to the output array which is an array of bytes (out_0, out_1,....out_{15}).

The formation of State at the beginning of the Cipher or Inverse Cipher from the input array *in* is done as follows:

$$S[r, c] = in[r + 4c] \qquad \text{for } 0 \leq r < 4 \text{ and } 0 \leq c < Nb, \quad (2.2)$$

At the end of the Cipher and Inverse Cipher the State is copied to the output array *out* as follows:

$$Out[r + 4c] = s[r, c] \qquad \text{for } 0 \leq c < Nb \text{ and } o \leq c < Nb. \quad (2.3)$$

2.5.2   The Algorithm Primitives:

The AES algorithm consists of the following operations [14][1]:

i.   The ByteSub Transformation:

The ByteSub Transformation is a nonlinear byte substitution operating on each of the State bytes independently. The substitution table (or S-box) is invertible and is constructed by initializing the table in ascending sequence row by row. Then, a composition of the following transformations is taken:

a. First, the multiplicative inverse in GF (2^8) is taken. The value of {00} is mapped to itself. The multiplication in $Gf(2^8)$ is described in (Appendix B).

b. Next, an affine-over GF (2)-transformation is applied. This is defined by :

$$y_i = x_i \oplus x_{(i+4)\text{mod}8} \oplus x_{(i+5)\text{mod}8} \oplus x_{(i+6)\text{mod}8} \oplus x_{(i+7)\text{mod}8} \oplus c_i \quad ....(2.4)$$

for $0 \leq i < 8$ where x_i is the ith bit of the input byte, y_i is the ith bit of the output byte and c_i is the ith bit of a byte c with the value {63}.

In matrix form the affine transformation of the S-box can be expressed as:

$$
\begin{bmatrix} y_0 \\ y_1 \\ y_2 \\ y_3 \\ y_4 \\ y_5 \\ y_6 \\ y_7 \end{bmatrix} = \begin{bmatrix} 1 & 0 & 0 & 0 & 1 & 1 & 1 & 1 \\ 1 & 1 & 0 & 0 & 0 & 1 & 1 & 1 \\ 1 & 1 & 1 & 0 & 0 & 0 & 1 & 1 \\ 1 & 1 & 1 & 1 & 0 & 0 & 0 & 1 \\ 1 & 1 & 1 & 1 & 1 & 0 & 0 & 0 \\ 0 & 1 & 1 & 1 & 1 & 1 & 0 & 0 \\ 0 & 0 & 1 & 1 & 1 & 1 & 1 & 0 \\ 0 & 0 & 0 & 1 & 1 & 1 & 1 & 1 \end{bmatrix} \begin{bmatrix} x_0 \\ x_1 \\ x_2 \\ x_3 \\ x_4 \\ x_5 \\ x_6 \\ x_7 \end{bmatrix} + \begin{bmatrix} 1 \\ 1 \\ 0 \\ 0 \\ 0 \\ 1 \\ 1 \\ 0 \end{bmatrix} \qquad \dots\dots(2.5)
$$

In figure (2.3) we illustrate the effect of the ByteSub transformation on the State.

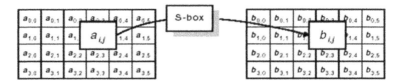

Figure (2.3): ByteSub acts on the individual bytes of the State.

The values of the S-box and the inverse S-box are shown in the Table (2.2) and Table (2.3) respectively.

Table (2.2): The values of the S-box

99	124	119	123	242	107	111	197	48	1	103	43	254	215	171	118
202	130	201	125	25	89	71	240	173	212	162	175	156	164	114	192
183	253	147	38	54	63	247	204	52	165	229	241	113	216	49	21
4	199	35	195	24	150	5	154	7	18	128	226	235	39	178	117
9	131	44	26	27	110	90	160	82	59	214	179	41	227	47	132
83	209	0	237	32	252	177	91	106	203	190	57	74	76	88	207
208	239	170	251	67	77	51	133	69	249	2	127	80	60	159	168
81	163	64	143	146	157	56	245	188	182	218	33	16	255	243	210
205	12	19	236	95	151	68	23	196	167	126	61	100	93	25	115
96	129	79	220	34	42	144	136	70	238	184	20	222	94	11	219
224	50	58	10	73	6	36	92	194	211	172	98	145	149	228	121
231	200	55	109	141	213	78	169	108	86	244	234	101	122	174	8
186	120	37	46	28	166	180	198	232	221	116	31	75	189	139	138
112	62	181	102	72	3	246	14	97	53	87	185	134	193	29	158
225	248	152	17	17	217	142	148	155	30	135	233	206	85	40	223
140	161	137	13	191	230	66	104	65	153	45	15	176	84	187	22

Table (2.3): The values of the inverted S-box

82	9	106	213	48	54	165	56	191	64	163	158	129	243	215	251
124	227	57	130	155	47	255	135	52	142	67	68	196	222	233	203
84	123	148	50	166	194	35	61	238	76	149	11	66	250	195	78
8	46	161	102	40	217	36	178	118	91	162	73	109	139	209	37
114	248	246	100	134	104	152	22	212	164	92	204	93	101	182	146
108	112	72	80	253	237	185	218	94	21	70	87	167	141	157	132
144	216	171	0	140	188	211	10	247	228	88	5	184	179	69	6
208	44	30	143	202	63	15	2	193	175	189	3	1	19	138	107
58	145	17	65	79	103	220	234	151	242	207	206	240	180	230	115
150	172	116	34	231	173	53	133	226	249	55	232	28	117	223	110
71	241	26	113	29	41	197	137	111	183	98	14	170	24	190	27
252	86	62	75	198	210	121	32	154	219	192	254	120	205	90	244
31	221	168	51	136	7	199	49	177	18	16	89	39	128	236	95
96	81	127	169	25	181	74	13	45	229	122	159	147	201	156	239
160	224	59	77	174	42	245	176	2	235	187	60	131	83	153	97
23	43	4	126	186	119	214	38	225	105	20	99	85	33	12	125

The inverse of ByteSub is the inverse byte substitution where the inverse table is applied. This is achieved by applying an inverse of the affine mapping followed by taking the multiplicative inverse in $GF(2^8)$ [16][1].

The inverted S-box appears in Table (2.3).

ii. The ShiftRow Transformation:

In ShiftRow, the rows of the State are cyclically shifted over different offsets. Row 0 is not shifted; Row 1 is shifted over C1 bytes, row 2 over C2 bytes and row 3 over C3 bytes. The shift offsets C1, C2 and C3 depend on the block length Nb. The offset values prespecified by the algorithm and are given in Table (2.4).

Table (2.4): Shift offsets for different block lengths.

Nb	C1	C2	C3
4	1	2	3
6	1	2	3
8	1	3	4

Figure (2.4) illustrates the effect of the ShiftRow transformation on the State.

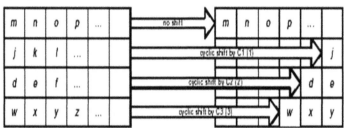

Figure (2.4): ShiftRow operating on the rows of State.

The inverse of ShiftRow is a cyclic shift of the three bottom rows over Nb-C1, Nb-C2 and Nb-C3 bytes respectively. Such that, the byte at position j in row i moves to position (j + Nb-Ci) mod Nb [16].

iii. The MixColumn Transformation:

In MixColumn, the columns of the State are considered as polynomials over GF (2^8). These polynomials are multiplied modulo x^4+1 with a fixed polynomial c(x) given by:

$$c(x) = \text{'03'}\, x^3 + \text{'01'}\, x^2 + \text{'01'}\, x^1 + \text{'02'}. \qquad .....(2.6).$$

This polynomial is co-prime to x^4+1 and therefore, inveritable. This can be written as a matrix multiplication [16][1]. Let b(x) =c(x) $\otimes$ a(x), be the MixColumn transformation of a(x):

$$\begin{bmatrix} b_0 \\ b_1 \\ b_2 \\ b_3 \end{bmatrix} = \begin{bmatrix} 02 & 03 & 01 & 01 \\ 01 & 02 & 03 & 01 \\ 01 & 01 & 02 & 03 \\ 03 & 01 & 01 & 02 \end{bmatrix} \begin{bmatrix} a_0 \\ a_1 \\ a_2 \\ a_3 \end{bmatrix} \qquad .....(2.7)$$

The way this transformation is applied to the State is shown in Figure (2.5):

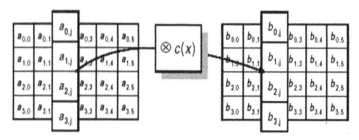

Figure (2.5): MixColumn operating on the columns of State.

The inverse of MixColumn is similar to MixColumn. Each column is transformed by multiplying it with a specific multiplication polynomial d(x), defined by:

$$('03' x^3 + '01' x^2 + '01' x + '02') \oplus d(x) = '01' \qquad ......(2.8).$$

d(X) is therefore given by:

$$d(x) = '0B' x^3 + '0D' x^2 + '09' x + '0E' \qquad ....(2.9).$$

iv. *The Round Key Addition:*

In this operation, a RoundKey is applied to State by a simple bitwise XOR. The RoundKey length is equal to the block length Nb. This transformation is illustrated in Figure (2.6).

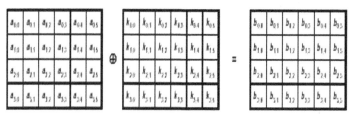

Figure (2.6): The key addition

v. *Key Schedule:*

The round keys are derived from the Cipher Key by means of the key schedule. This consists of two components: the Key Expansion and the RoundKey Selection.

The basic principles in deriving the key are [14]:

19

a. The total number of RoundKey bits is equal to the block length multiplied by the number of rounds plus 1. That's, for a block length of 128 bits and 10 rounds, 1408 RoundKey bits are needed.
b. The cipher key is expanded into an expanded key.
c. RoundKeys are taken from the expanded key in the following way: the first RoundKey consists of the first Nb words, the second one of the following Nb words, and so on.

vi. *Key Expansion:*

The Expanded Key is a linear array of 4-byte words and is denoted by W[Nb*(Nr+1)]. The first Nk words contain the Cipher Key. All the other words are derived recursively.

The key expansion function depends on the value of Nk. There is a version of this function for Nk less than or equal 6, and another version for Nk above 6. The code for the key expansion function for Nk $\leq$ 6 is given below [1]:

```
KeyExpansion (byte Key [4*Nk] word W [Nb*(Nr+1)])
{
        for (i = 0; i < Nk; i++)
        W[i] = (Key [4*i], Key [4*i+1], Key [4*i+2], Key [4*i+3]);
        for (i = Nk; i < Nb * (Nr + 1); i++)
            {
                    temp = W [i - 1];
                    if (I % No == 0)
                    temp = SubByte (RotByte (temp)) ^ Rcon [i / Nk];
                    W[i] = W [i - Nk] ^ temp;
            }
}
```

In the above algorithm, SubByte(W) is a function that returns a 4-byte word in which each byte is the result of applying the Rijndael S-box to the byte at the corresponding position in the input word.

The function RotByte(W) returns a word in which the bytes are the cyclic permutation of those in its input such that the input word (a, b, c, d) produces the output word (b, c, d, a). It can be seen that the first Nk words are filled with the Cipher Key.

Every following word W[i] is the result of XORing the previous word W [i-1] and the word Nk positions earlier (W [i-Nk]). For words in positions that are a multiple of Nk a transformation is applied to W[i-1] followed by XORing with a round constant. This transformation consists of a cyclic shift of the bytes in the word (RotByte) followed by the application of a table lookup to all four bytes of the word (SubByte). The code for the key expansion function for Nk > 6 is given below [1]:

KeyExpansion (byte Key [4*Nk] word W [Nb*(Nr+1)])
{
    for (i = 0; i < Nk; i++)
    W [i] = (key [4*i], key [4*i+1], key [4*i+2], key [4*i+3]);
    for (i = No; i < Nb * (Nr + 1); i++)
        {
            temp = W [i - 1];
            if (i % Nk == 0)
                temp = SubByte (RotByte (temp)) ^ Rcon [i / Nk];
            else if (i % Nk == 4)
                temp = SubByte (temp);
            W [i] = W [i - Nk] ^ temp;
        }
}

The difference of this procedure with the scheme for Nk ≤ 6 is that for [i-4] a multiple of Nk SubByte is applied to W [i-1] prior to the XOR.

The round constants are independent of Nk and are defined by:

$$Rcon[i] = (RC [i], `00', `00', `00')$$

With RC[i] representing an element in GF (2^8) with a value of $x^{(i-1)}$ so that:

$$RC [1] = 1 \text{ (i.e. `01')} \qquad\qquad\qquad ....(2.10)$$
$$RC[i] = x \text{ (i.e. `02')} \cdot (RC [i-1]) = x^{(i-1)} \qquad\qquad ....(2.11)$$

vii. Round Key Selection:

The key for round *i* is selected from the RoundKey bank of key words in the range from W [Nb*i] to W[Nb*(i+1)]. This is illustrated in Figure (2.7).

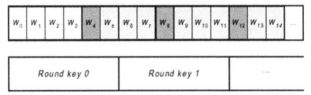

Figure (2.7): RoundKey selection for Nb=6 and Nk=4.

2.5.3   The Encryption Process:

The encryption procedure by using Rijndael algorithm consists of:

  a. An initial Round Key addition.
  b. Nr-1 Rounds.
  c. A final round.

The entire encryption process is illustrated in the algorithm show in Figure (2.8).

2.5.4   The Decryption Process:

The decryption process in Rijndael runs the encryption process in reverse order. Transformations are replaced with their inverse counterparts. Figure (2.9) shows both encryption and decryption procedures with the individual operations aligned to their inverse

2.6 A Worked Example:

To show the operation of the Rijndael encryption algorithm a text statement will be used as an input to the algorithm. The letters of the text message are converted into their numeric ASCII code equivalents. The algorithm is implemented by using MATLAB® code.

The code is first organized in columns to form the State matrix ready to be encrypted. The detailed intermediated results of the encryption process is given in appendix A.

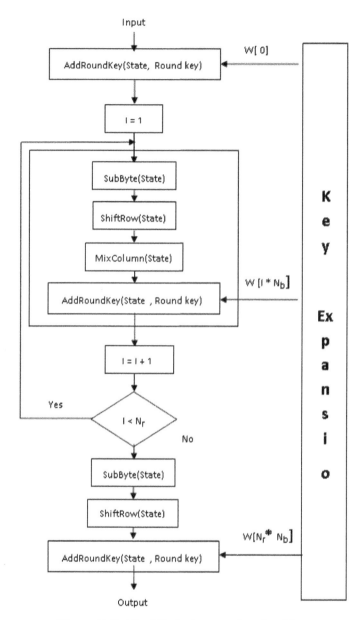

Figure (2.8): The Rijndael encryption algorithm.

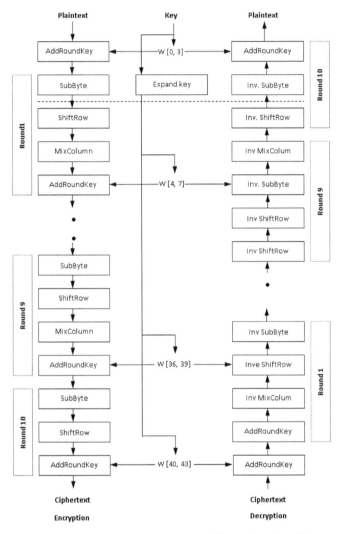

Figure (2.9) Rijndael encryption and decryption algorithms.

The input statement to the Rijndael algorithm is given below:

Republic Of Iraq

Initially, the ASCII code equivalents of the statement (in Hex.) is computed and organized in columns:

$$
\begin{array}{cccc}
52 & 62 & 20 & 49 \\
65 & 6c & 4f & 75 \\
70 & 69 & 66 & 61 \\
75 & 63 & 20 & 71 \\
\end{array}
$$

The encryption key is initialized (in Hex) as follows:

$$
\begin{array}{cccc}
00 & 44 & 88 & cc \\
11 & 55 & 99 & dd \\
22 & 66 & aa & ee \\
33 & 77 & bb & ff \\
\end{array}
$$

The values of State during the last round of the algorithm are listed below:

State at start of final round

$$
\begin{array}{cccc}
7b & b4 & c7 & 39 \\
8b & 89 & d7 & 44 \\
f5 & 29 & e6 & a2 \\
d0 & 62 & c5 & 88 \\
\end{array}
$$

After SubByte

$$
\begin{array}{cccc}
21 & 8d & c6 & 12 \\
3d & a7 & 0e & 1b \\
e6 & a5 & 8e & 3a \\
70 & aa & a6 & c4 \\
\end{array}
$$

After ShiftRow

$$
\begin{array}{cccc}
21 & 8d & c6 & 12 \\
a7 & 0e & 1b & 3d \\
8e & 3a & e6 & a5 \\
c4 & 70 & aa & a6 \\
\end{array}
$$

Round key

25

```
36  1d  5f  4c
d0  84  c0  ba
24  b8  f9  b6
46  37  c0  bb
```

Final state :
```
17  90  99  5e
77  8a  db  87
aa  82  1f  13
82  47  6a  1d
```

The output Cipher (in Hex):
```
17  90  99  5e
77  8a  db  87
aa  82  1f  13
82  47  6a  1d
```

3

Host FPGA Platform

3.1 Introduction:

There are many programmable devices (PD) and similarly different methods for their categorization. Some of these classification methods depend on the IC's semiconductor technology, vaulted and non-vaulted, programmability, flexibility, capacity, routing method or the characteristics of basic cell (core logic circuit) [17].

The classification that depends on the characteristics of the basic cell is the most important one. The approach is usually called virtual classification [18]. The cell characteristics determine the kind of function suitable for that particular programmable device [17].

In addition those characteristics give a simple and understandable model of realization of complex circuits on host FPGA platform such as Xilinx's or Altera's or etc. Then, the use of this model is to give the general rules of the conventional circuit design and optimization using the host FPGA.

This approach ensures the design is reusable with the other sister platforms. It is accepted that these rules will help the designer to implement circuits with optimal cost and performance characteristics [17].

3.2 *General Classification of PDs:*

There are many programmable devices that can be used in the implementation of digital signal processing (DSP) systems and functions. Two main types of them depend on the function of their cells (virtual classification). Figure (3.1) shows some of the common programmable devices [17][19][20].

Most DSP systems use the gate cell approach because of their capability to reduce the Boolean expressions of the DSP circuits. Programmable Logic Arrays (PLA) and Programmable Array Logic (PAL) have low flexibility and low capacity (maximum

32 inputs and 32 outputs) they are therefore, used in small DSP circuits implementations [16][20].

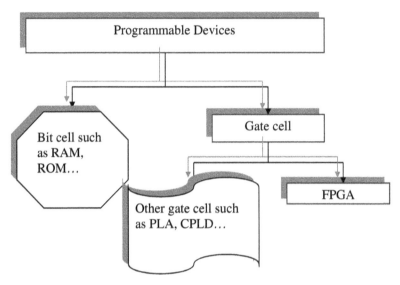

Figure (3.1): Virtual classification of programmable devices.

The Complex Programmable Logic Device (CPLD) is the first generation of the Field Programmable Gate Array (FPGA). This type of programmable device has high flexibility but low capacity. It is used to implement small and medium systems with small control circuits [21].

FPGA is a relatively new addition to the programmable devices family. It has higher flexibility and a different internal architecture which depends on the manufacturing company (e.g. Altera, Actel, Xilinx… etc). However, what's common feature among these devices is the availability of a set of free or semi-free connection matrix gates [22].

According to the so-called virtual classification of FPGAs (as shown in Figure (3.2)), these devices can be divided into two categories: fine-grain logic blocks such as Algotronix, Concurrent Logic, Plessey and Toshiba and coarse-grain logic blocks such as Actel, Altera, and Xilinx [23] depending on their particular size.

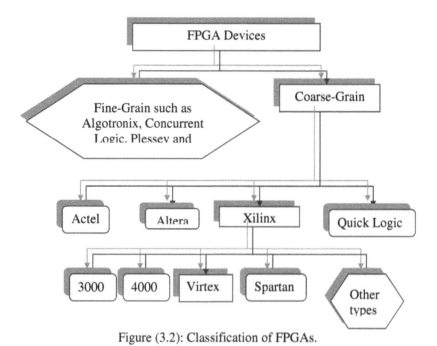

Figure (3.2): Classification of FPGAs.

3.3 The Xilinx® Logic Block:

The basis for the Xilinx logic block is an SRAM functioning as a look-up table (LUT). The truth table for K-input logic function is stored in a 2^K SRAM. The address lines of the SRAM are used as inputs, while the output of the SRAM provides the value of the logic function [25].

The advantage of the look-up tables (LUT) is that they provide high functionality while being extremely simple and infinitely reprogrammable. A K-input LUT can implement any function of K inputs and there are 2^{2^K} such functions.

The main disadvantage of using LUT is that they will be quite large for tables with more than five inputs [25]. This is because the number of memory cells needed has to be doubled for each extra input.

3.4 *Architecture of Virtex-E:*

The Virtex-E FPGA shown in Figure (3.3) comprises three major configurable elements: configurable logic blocks (CLBs), input/output blocks (IOBs) and general routing matrix (GRM) [1].

a) CLBs provide the functional elements for constructing logic.
b) IOBs provide the interface between the package pins and the CLBs.
c) GRM interconnects the CLBs.

The GRM comprises an array of routing switches located at the intersections of horizontal and vertical routing channels. Each CLB nests into a Versa Ring block that provides local routing resources to connect the CLB to the GRM [25][26].

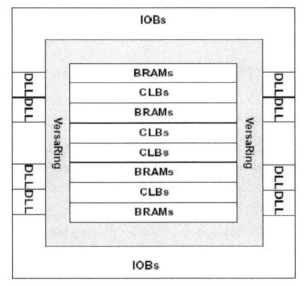

Figure (3.3): Virtex-E Architecture Overview.

The Versa Ring I/O interface provides additional routing resources around the periphery of the device. This routing improves I/O routability and facilitates pin locking.

The Virtex-E package also includes the following circuits which are connected to the GRM [26]:

1. Dedicated block memories (BRAMs) of 4096 bits for each block.
2. Clock DLLs for clock-distribution delay compensation and clock domain control.
3. Tri-State buffers (BUFTs) associated with each CLB that drive dedicated segmentable horizontal routing resources.

Values stored in static memory cells control the configurable logic elements and interconnect resources. These values are loaded into the memory cells on power-up, and can be reloaded if necessary to change the function of the device.

I/O block (IOB) in the Virtex-E selects inputs and outputs that support a wide variety of I/O signaling standards. There are three IOB storage elements as shown in Figure (3.4). They work either as edge-triggered D-type flip-flops or as level-sensitive latches.

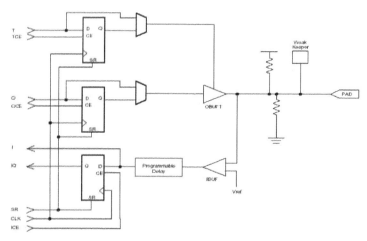

Figure (3.4): Virtex-E Input/Output Block (IOB).

Each IOB has a clock signal (CLK) shared by the three flip-flops as well as independent clock enable signals for each flip-flop [26]. In addition to the CLK and CE control signals, the three flip-flops share a Set/Reset (SR). For each flip-flop this signal can be independently configured as a synchronous set, a synchronous reset, an asynchronous preset, or an asynchronous clear.

The output buffer and all of the IOB control signals have independent polarity controls [26]. Input path in the Virtex-E IOB routes the input signal directly to internal logic and/or through an optional input flip-flop. On the other hand, the output path includes a 3-state output buffer that drives the output signal onto the pad.

The output signal can be routed to the buffer directly from the internal logic or through an optional IOB output flip-flop. The 3-state control of the output can also be routed directly from the internal logic or through a flip-flop that provides synchronous enable and disable [26][27].

3.5 Xilinx FPGA CLB Structure:

The basic building block of the Virtex-E configurable logic block is the logic cell (LC). An LC includes a 4-input function generator, carry logic and a storage element. The output from the function generator in each LC drives both the CLB output and the D input of the flip-flop. The internal structure of the logic block is shown in Figure (3.5).

Each Virtex-E CLB contains four LCs organized in two similar slices as shown in Figure (3.6). In addition to the four basic LCs, the Virtex-E CLB contains logic that combines function generators to provide functions of five or six inputs. Consequently, when estimated, the number of system gates provided by a given device in each CLB counts as 4 LCs [26][28].

Virtex-E function generators are implemented as 4-input look-up tables (LUTs). In addition to its operation as a function generator each LUT can provide a 16 x 1-bit synchronous RAM.

Furthermore, the two LUTs within a slice can be combined to create a 16 x 2-bit or 32 x 1-bit synchronous RAM, or a 16x1-bit dual-port synchronous RAM.

As shown in Figure (3.6) the F5 input in each slice combines the two function generators in the slice. This combination provides either a function generator that can implement any 5-input function, a 4:1 multiplexer, or select functions of up to nine inputs.

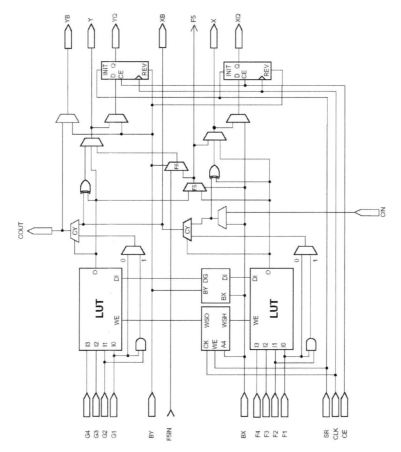

Figure (3.5): Internal organization of Virtex-E Slice.

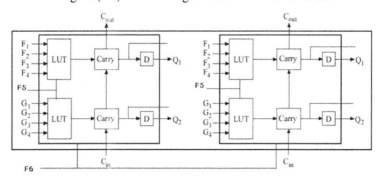

Figure (3.6): A simplified structure of Virtex- E CLB.

33

In a similar way, the F6 input combines the outputs of all four-function generators in the CLB by selecting one of the F5-multiplexer outputs. This permits the implementation of any 6-input function, an 8:1 multiplexer, or selects functions of up to 19 inputs.

Each CLB has four direct feed through paths, two per slice. These paths provide extra data input lines or additional local routing that does not consume logic resources [26].

3.6 Circuit Design with Virtex-E:

The characteristics of Xilinx Virtex-E FPGA can give a set of rules to implement optimal circuits. That's to reduce the cost and increase the speed of target circuit. These rules differ from those that have already been used in simplifying Boolean expressions.

The guidelines of implementation for an optimal cost and a high-speed system in Virtex-E Xilinx FPGA can be summarized here [25]:

a) Divide the large number of inputs circuit to small sub circuits with the number of inputs less than 7-input in each logic equation. Otherwise, the design of a function of large number of inputs will be uncontrollable in space and time delay design. Where the space and speed of the circuits implemented by Virtex-E Xilinx FPGA depend on the number of inputs and are independent of the complexity of logic equations. The cost of each circuit can be calculated as follows [25]:

$$Cost = \begin{cases} 2^{(n-4)} & \text{for } n > 4 \\ 1 & \text{for } n \leq 4 \end{cases} \qquad (3.1)$$

where n is the number of inputs in the circuit. The delay on the other hand can be calculated as follows:

$$Delay \quad = \quad \left\lceil \frac{n}{6} \right\rceil \qquad (3.2)$$

This means that a Boolean equation which has less than 6-input needs one unit delay and those equations with 7-input to 36-input need two unit delays and so on.

34

b) Four-input equations in sub-circuits give a minimum cost because each such function needs one cell and one unit delay. However, such circuits will have a large number of cells that are connected in series. This will consequently increases the total delay.

c) Six-input equations in sub-circuits give the maximum speed because each such function needs four cells (one whole CLB) and one unit delay. However, such circuits will have a small number of cells that are connected in series. This in turn decreases the total delay and may increase the total cost.

d) Five-input equations in sub-circuits give an optimal cost and speed. This is because each 5-input function needs two cells and one unit delay.

It is clear that the restriction of six-input function should be abided to as possible. This is because each seven-input function needs eight cells and two unit delays. Similarly, one-input, two-input, and three-input functions need one cell and one unit delay.

3.7 Circuit Design with Virtex-II:

Similarly, as with the Virtex-E Xilinx FPGA the characteristics of Xilinx Virtex-II FPGA give a set of rules. These rules help to implement with optimal cost and speed in Virtex-II FPGA. These rules are listed below:

a) Divide the large number of inputs circuit to small sub circuits with the number of inputs less than 8-input in each logic equation. As with Virtex-E the space and speed of the circuits implemented by Virtex-II FPGA depend on the number of inputs and are independent of the complexity of logic equations. The cost of each circuit can be calculated by using equation (3.1) [25]. The delay can be computed by using equation (3.3):

$$Delay \quad = \quad \left\lceil \frac{n}{7} \right\rceil \qquad (3.3)$$

where n is the number of inputs. This means that the Boolean equation which has less than 7-input needs one unit delay and those with 8-input to 49-input need two unit delays and so on.

35

b) Four-input equations in sub-circuits give minimum cost because each such function needs one cell and one unit delay. However, such circuits will have a large number of cells that are connected in series. This increases the total delay.

c) Five-input equations in sub circuits give an optimal cost/speed. This is due to the fact that each 5-input function needs two cells and one unit delay.

d) Six-input equations in-sub circuits give an optimal speed but higher cost than the 5-input case. This is because each 6-input function needs four cells and one unit delay.

e) Seven-input equations in sub-circuits give the maximum speed, because each 7-input function needs eight cells (one CLB) and one unit delay. However, such circuits have a small number of cells that are connected in series. Eventually decreasing the total delay but increasing the total cost.

f) It must be mentioned that there are additional advantages of Virtex-II over Virtex-E series, these advantages inclue:

i. Virtex-II requires one cell to implement two neighbor functions if the first is asynchrony and the second is buffer. This is because of the possibility to separate the LUT and the D flip-flop in the same cell.

ii. A single term function that has 5-to-10 inputs requires two cells and one unit delay. Hence, a single term function that has 11-to-18 inputs will require four cells and one unit delay. However, a single term function that has 19-to-35 inputs will require eight cells and one unit delay.

iii. The MUX architecture functions of less than 16 inputs require one cell and one unit delay. As an example, a 3 inputs (A, B, S) MUX function has the form:

$$F=SA + S\bar{B}.$$

It is clear that the restriction of seven-input function must be observed as possible. This is because each 8-input function needs sixteen cells and two-unit delay. As before, 1-input, 2-input and 3-input functions require one cell and one unit delay.

3.8 VHDL Language:

Programmable devices need a programming language to convert the system design to a suitable code, test this design and transfer it to the hardware map in the programmed devices.

One of most used language to program FPGA devices is the **VHSIC** **H**ardware **D**escription **L**anguage (**VHDL**). The acronym **V**HSIC refers to **V**ery **H**igh-**S**peed **I**ntegrated **C**ircuit [31].

There are numerous development software packages used to model with VHDL for such as ModelSim and etc. ModelSim gives the capability to examine realistic timing for all signals of components implemented in VHDL code. This is an important feature to use before converting design into hardware map [32].

The software package Xilinx ISE 4.1i can convert the VHDL code to hardware map. It also provides space report of internal connection and timing report for FPGA chip with an accuracy of more than 95% compared to actual implementation parameters.

VHDL can be regarded as integrated amalgamation of the following languages [33]:

a) Sequential language +
b) Concurrent language +
c) net-list language +
d) timing specifications +
e) waveform generation language

Evidently, VHDL incorporates constructs that enable to express the concurrent or sequential behavior of a digital system with or without timing. It also allows for modeling a system as an interconnection of components. Test waveforms can also be generated by using same constructs. These constructs can actually be combined to provide a comprehensive description of the system in a single model.

3.9 VHDL Specifics:

VHDL is virtually the ultimate tool for programming with FPGA. This in particular is due to the set of features and capabilities that the language offer and differentiate it from other languages. These features are summarized below [33]:

a) The language can be used as an exchange medium between chip vendors and CAD (computer aided design) tool users.
b) The language can also be used as a communication medium between different CAD and CAE (computer aided engineering) tools.

c) The language supports hierarchy. That is, a digital system can be modeled as a set of interconnected components, each in turn, can be modeled as a set of interconnected subcomponents.

d) The language is not technology-specific, but is capable of supporting technology-specific features.

e) It supports both synchronous and asynchronous timing models.

f) Various digital modeling techniques, such as finite-state machine descriptions, algorithmic descriptions, and Boolean equations can be modeled by using the language.

g) VHDL is publicly available, human-readable, machine-readable, and above all, it is not proprietary.

h) It is an IEEE and ANSI standard. Therefore, models described by using this language are portable.

i) VHDL supports both all basic different description styles: structural, data flow and behavioral.

j) It supports a wide range of abstraction levels ranging from abstract behavioral descriptions to very precise gate level descriptions.

k) Arbitrarily large designs can be modeled by using VHDL and there are no limitations imposed by language on the size of a design.

l) The language has elements that make large-scale design modeling easier, such as components, functions, procedures, and packages.

m) Test benches can be written by using the same language to test other VHDL models.

n) Nominal propagation delay, min-max delays, setup and hold timing, timing constraints and spike detection can all be described very naturally in this language.

o) The use of generics and attributes in the models facilitate backannotation of static information such as timing or placement information.

p) Generics and attributes are also useful in describing parameterized designs.

q) Models written in VHDL can be verified by simulation since precise simulation semantics are defined for each language construct.

4

Rijndael Implementation on Xilinx®
Platforms

4.1 Introduction:

The implementation issue being the core of this study comes after a significant discussion of the target algorithm as well as the host technology. The main subject of this chapter is the employment of the previously stated rules and ideas as the basis of the implementation operation. This chapter deals with the algorithm as a set of sequential operations

4.2 FPGA Pipelining:

The encryption algorithm as mentioned in chapter 2 can be implemented with ten rounds. Each round consists of four stages (operations) except for the last round which has only three operations.

Since the algorithm is proposed for implementation on the Xilinx® platforms, therefore, the internal organization of the host FPGA is considered to guide the design process. This is achieved by using the rules discussed earlier to optimize the design map towards high speed and low cost.

FPGA platforms like the Xilinx technology proposed here can be maximally utilized by adopting a piplined designs approach. The easiest way to think of this design is by taking each stage (operation) per single round and converting it to a pipeline stage. This procedure is shown in Figure (4.1).

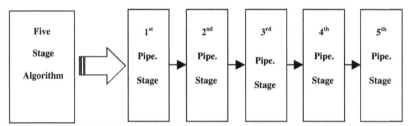

Figure (4.1): Direct mapping of Rijndael stages into pipeline.

This breaking of the original algorithm in several pipline stages is valid for symmetrically lengthed (with equal delay) stages. It's worth mentioning that such feature is not always available in the algorithm to be implemented. Rijndael's is a prime example because its original operations happen to have different lengths.

Hence, some efforts have to be invested in order to make full use of the efficient pipelining approach. This is basically done by partitioning the lengthy stages in the original algorithm into two or more new sub-stages while preserving the functionality. This approach is depicted in Figure (4.2).

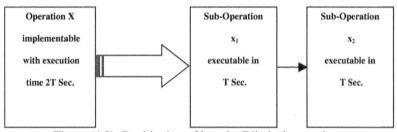

Figure (4.2): Partitioning of lengthy Rijndael operations

The fragmentation of large operations into smaller sub-operations to be of value is carried on along all the stages and rounds of the algorithm. Practically, in our proposed design, partitioning of stages has resulted in halving the delay. This consequently resulted in doubling the operational speed.

Needless to say that increasing the operational frequency can sometimes be by itself the goal. This is irrespective of whither this is accompanied by increasing the throughput or not. This is particularly true when the system is required to be synchronized with other systems.

As for the cost issue, partitioning results in a better and more controlled size requirements if compared with the un-partitioned implementation of the algorithm. These points will be further touched upon in the subsequent sections as appropriate.

4.3 Encryption Implementation:

The implementation of stages of encryption algorithm is discussed in the subsequent sections:

4.3.1 ByteSub Implementation:

This operation can be considered as the most problematic stage. This is due to the function included being byte oriented table look-up operation. The operation is implemented such that the input byte is used as an address to a pre-stored value.

The difficulty here arises upon trying to synchronize this stage with the successive and (after the first round) the previous stages in the pipeline. This is because in this stage eight bits must be transformed into their equivalent values in one clock. Attempting to do so conflicts with the rules of chapter 3 hence, resulting in uncontrollable in space and delay parameters.

Subtable 0
Subtable 1
Subtable 2
Subtable 3

Figure (4.3): Look-up table partitioning

To alleviate this bottleneck, the design proposes the following compromise: the transformation table is subdivided into four sub-tables as shown in Figure (4.3). Lookup tables LUT0, LUT1, LUT2, and LUT3are then created each of which is with six-bit entries as shown below:

41

LUT0	00XXXXXX
LUT1	01XXXXXX
LUT2	10XXXXXX
LUT3	11XXXXXX

This step has two benefits: first it is implementable with maximum speed since it needs one unit delay and second, no more than one CLB for each bit to be implemented. The output of these sub-stages (look-up tables) is then to stored rather than fed directly to the next stage. The above description is summarized by the following formula:

$$\text{Sub} = (\neg \text{bit5} \wedge \neg \text{bit4} \wedge \text{LUT0}) \vee (\neg \text{bit5} \wedge \text{bit4} \wedge \text{LUT1}) \vee (\text{bit5} \wedge \neg \text{bit4} \wedge \text{LUT2}) \vee (\text{bit5} \wedge \text{bit4} \wedge \text{LUT3}) \qquad \ldots\ldots(4.1)$$

where "$\neg$" NOT, "$\wedge$" AND, and "$\vee$" OR are the logical operators. Sub is the resultant byte of this sub-table transformation. The intermediate result is written as Sub0, Sub1, Sub2, and Sub3 for sub-tables 0, 1, 2, and 3 respectively.

Now, these tables can be realized on Xilinx® FPGA by involving one CLB as follows:

i.   The four least significant bits (bit0-bit3) of the input byte become indices to the contents of the four LCs, as shown in Figure (4.4).

ii.   The outputs of the two LCs in each slice are fed to the input of the multiplexer F5.

iii. The fifth bit (bit4) is fed to the *select* input of the two F5 of the CLB.

iv.   The outputs of the two F5 multiplexers are fed to the two inputs of the multiplexer F6.

v.   The sixth bit (bit5) is connected to the *select* input of F6 multiplexer.

vi.   The output of F6 is connected to the input of the D-flip flop. From which the final output of the CLB will be taken after each clock triggers that flip flop.

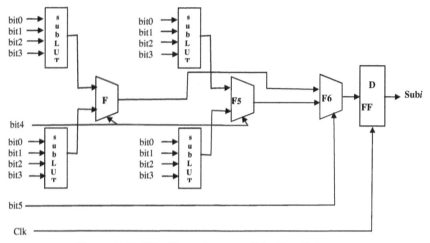

Figure (4.4): The first sub-stage of the ByteSub stage.

This is the end of the first sub-stage of the ByteSub transformation. The output from the four sub-tables (Sub0, Sub1, Sub2, and Sub3) together with the two index bits (bit6 and bit7) of the input byte form a six bits function. The formula for this function is given below:

$$\textbf{SubByte} = (\neg \textbf{bit7} \wedge \neg \textbf{bit6} \wedge \textbf{Sub0}) \vee (\neg \textbf{bit7} \wedge \textbf{bit6} \wedge \textbf{Sub1}) \vee (\textbf{bit7} \wedge \neg \textbf{bit6} \wedge \textbf{Sub2}) \vee (\textbf{bit7} \wedge \textbf{bit6} \wedge \textbf{Sub3}) \quad .....(4.2)$$

where, as before, "¬" NOT, "∧" AND, and "∨" OR are the logical operators. The SubByte variable in this function represents the output of the ByteSub transformation.

The way in which we implement the above equation is by using the Sub0, Sub1, Sub2, and Sub3 as inputs to each of the four LCs of the CL as shown in Figure (4.5).

The outputs of the two LCs of the first slice are fed to multiplexer F5 and bit6 is used as the *select* to this multiplexer. The same is done for the second slice of the CLB. The outputs from the two multiplexers are fed to the input of multiplexer F6.

When *select* is connected to bit7 the output of F6 is stored in the D-flip flop. The output is generated after triggering the next clock. This represents the end of the second sub-stage of the ByteSub transformation.

43

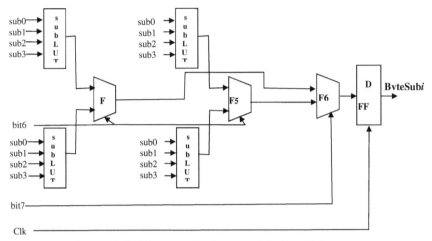

Figure (4.5): The second substage of the ByteSub stage.

The above described organization uses two LCs by two stages per bit, two F5 multiplexers, and an F6 multiplexer. Also, the delay per stage is one unit. Direct placement of the table contents on the other hand uses on rough estimation three CLBs, six F5 multiplexers and three F6 multiplexers. In addition, the total delay would be more than three units, let alone the long serial path the data take to reach final point as a transformed output. Thus, it can be concluded that the proposed implementation reduces the cost to one third and increases the speed three times.

This organization gives its best results with piplined architecture and produces the highest throughput when the pipe fills with data.

4.3.2   ShiftRow Implementation:

From the point of view of implementation on Xilinx® FPGA the ShiftRow costs very few resources as shown in Figure (4.6). In addition to the (almost) freely provided wiring it needs an isolating layer of clocked buffers to prevent the shifted data from passing to the next stage (MixColumn) before the arrival of the next clock. This is in part to preserve the structure and abide by the pipelining rules. This also ensures that the design is of high speed and throughput.

Thus to implement this stage the output bytes of the ByteSub stages are each shifted accordingly. This is done with no more than changing data indices. These

44

bytes are then stored in the D-flip flops of the corresponding CLBs. The remaining logic resources in the used CLB can be used by the compiler for some other tasks.

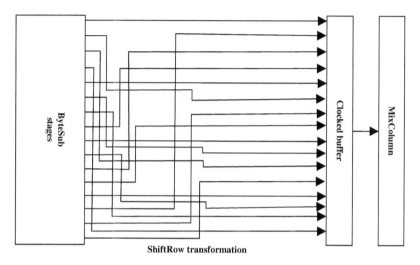

Figure (4.6): The implementation of ShiftRow transformation.

4.3.3   MixColumn Implementation:

This operation is to some extent complex and requires the use of finite fields multiplication. Further details regarding multiplication in Gf can be found in appendix B.

The assumed complexity in theoretical basis is related also directly to the implementation issue especially low level (gate level) hardware implementations. This operation manipulates the State matrix column by column treating each one as a four term polynomial over Gf (2^8). The operation multiplies them modulo (X^4+1) with a fixed polynomial a(X) [11]:

$$a(X) = \{03\} X^3+\{01\}X^2+\{01\}X+\{02\} \qquad (4.1)$$

The multiplication in equation (4.2):

$$S'(r,c)=a(r,c) \bullet S(r,c) \qquad (4.2)$$

can be represented in matrix form, as shown in equation (4.3):

45

$$
\begin{bmatrix} s'_{0,c} \\ s'_{1,c} \\ s'_{2,c} \\ s'_{3,c} \end{bmatrix}
=
\begin{bmatrix} 02 & 03 & 01 & 01 \\ 01 & 02 & 03 & 01 \\ 01 & 01 & 02 & 03 \\ 03 & 01 & 01 & 02 \end{bmatrix}
\bullet
\begin{bmatrix} s_{0,c} \\ s_{1,c} \\ s_{2,c} \\ s_{3,c} \end{bmatrix}
\qquad .....(4.3)
$$

Thus, the operation can be represented as in equation (4.4):

$$S'_{0,c} = (\{02\} \bullet S_{0,c}) \oplus (\{03\} \bullet S_{1,c}) \oplus S_{2,c} \oplus S_{3,c} \; .$$

$$S'_{1,c} = S_{0,c} \oplus (\{02\} \bullet S_{1,c}) \oplus (\{03\} \bullet S_{2,c}) \oplus S_{3,c}.$$

$$S'_{2,c} = S_{0,c} \oplus S_{1,c} \oplus (\{02\} \bullet S_{0,2}) \oplus (\{03\} \bullet S_{3,c}) \; .$$

$$S'_{3,c} = (\{03\} \bullet S_{0,c}) \oplus S_{1,c} \oplus S_{2,c} \oplus (\{02\} \bullet S_{3,c}) \; .$$

$$..... (4.4)$$

The above equations open the way for suggesting an interesting implementation strategy. The equations state that there are a byte oriented XOR and a multiplication in Gf (2^8). From knowledge of finite field multiplication the multiplication by two is simply a shift operation also known as xtime function (see appendix B).

There is also the requirement of XORing the resulting (shifted) byte with the constant polynomial m(x) $= x^8 + x^4 + x^3 + x + 1$ (reduction) in case of overflow. Otherwise, the result is already in the reduced form.

Now, since by definition the highest multiplication in this operation is by three. Therefore, there will be no need for more than one shift (for multiplication by two). This is followed by XORing with the original byte (for multiplication by three).

Hence, putting these facts together gives the following flow of events:

i. The bytes to be multiplied by one are kept unchanged until step IV.

ii. The bytes to be multiplied by two are shifted according to the xtime function (appendix B).

iii. The bytes to be multiplied by three are shifted according to the xtime function. The result should be XORed with the original (unshifted) byte later on step v.

iv. The non-reduced results are flagged in order to be reduced on step v below.

v. This is the XOR operation step where the XORs mentioned in Equation (4.4), the XOR mentioned in step iii and the XOR mentioned in step IV are all performed in one shot.

Figure (4.7) depicts the algorithmic logical flow of instances defining collectively the MixColumn operation.

Careful inspection of the above mentioned steps and figure together with the architectural considerations of the Xilinx® FPGAs leads to the decision of partitioning this stage as shown in Figure (4.8). Therefore, implementation wise, this stage is subdivided into two stages as follows:

The most significant bits of the bytes to be multiplied by two and three are both XORed and stored as a flag. (This is the end of the first sub stage):

i. If the flag is one then one of the two bytes (when shifted) would have an overflow (non-reduced) therefore, needs to be reduced. Thus, the m(x) variables in the next sub-stage must be equal to $x^8+x^4+x^3+x+1$.

ii. If the flag is zero then either none or both of the bytes to be shifted would have an overflow.

Since XORing a byte with all zeros makes no change for that byte and since XORing a byte with itself gives all zeros (under control of flag), therefore, if the shifted result for both bytes is reduced then XORing with zeros makes no change.

If they both are non-reduced, then, XORing the reduction polynomial m(x) with itself results in all zeros polynomial byte.

The second sub- stage involves XORing the six variables, the non-multiplied byte, the shifted byte (to be multiplied by two), the shifted byte (to be multiplied by three), the unshifted byte (to be multiplied by three) and the m(x) polynomial.

In addition to storage for input byte the first sub stage needs one slice to perform the XOR operation that results in the flag.

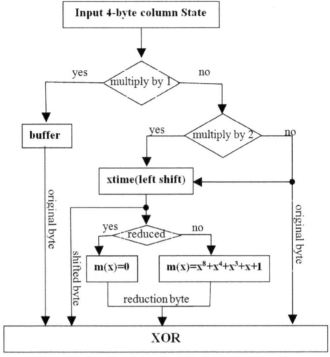

Figure (4.7): Algorithm for MixColumn operation.

It must be mentioned here that the compiler has to be forced to use a slice and not a cell by making the XOR operation look like (bit7 $\oplus$ bit6 $\oplus$ 0 $\oplus$ 0 $\oplus$ 0). This would conform to the rule (d) in section (3.5) for optimal cost/speed.

The second sub stage receives its six input variables on the next clock and uses one CLB to perform the XOR on these variables. The next clock indicates the end of the current MixColumn operation.

4.3.4 AddRoundKey Implementation:

The round key addition is performed by applying a bitwise XORing of the State with the round key. For implementation issues it is sometimes important to sacrifice in one aspect to avoid degraded results on other aspects. This is fact as appears below is evident in this stage.

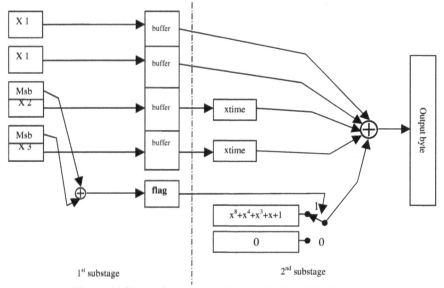

Figure (4.8): Implementation (logical) of the MixColumn.

This operation can be implemented by using an XOR instruction between the input state and the key bits. The implementation can be by using one cell per bit. This is very good for space but not for speed. That is why a small but important modification needs to be performed here.

This modification involves instructing the compiler to XOR the input and the key bits together with three zeros. The choice of zeros has the benefit of unchanging the result of XOR operation.

The number of zeros with the original operands counts five. Hence, complying with the rule (d) in section (3.5) where each bit XOR uses one slice, as shown in Figure (4.9).

4.4 Implementation of Decryption:

The stages of decryption are detailed in the subsequent sections.

4.4.1 InvByteSub Implementation:

The implementation of this stage is the same as that of ByteSub (section 4.3.1).

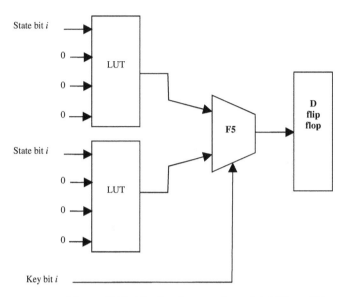

Figure (4.9): The implementation of AddRoundKey.

4.4.2 InvShiftRow Implementation:

This stage is simply the direct inverse (reverse) of the ShiftRow stage (encryption). It has the same specifications and consuming the same resources but differs in the indexing (the routing) details.

The new routing map for decryption is depicted in Figure (4.10) where the output of the InvByteSub is directed according to this stage rules and then the InvShifted bytes would be stored in clocked buffers. From which they will be available for use by InvMixColumn on the next clock (piplining requirements).

4.4.3 InvMixColumn Implementation:

This operation has the same basis for MixColumn but with more complexity and more stages for implementation. The operation is represented as follows [11]:-

$$a^{-1}(x)=\{0b\}x^3+\{0d\}x^2+\{09\}x+\{0e\} \tag{4.9}$$

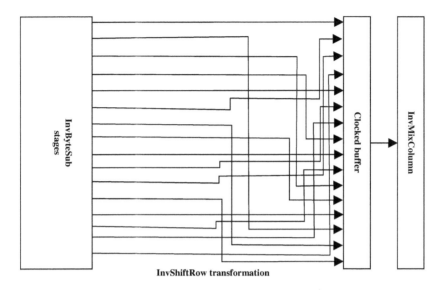

InvShiftRow transformation

Figure (4.10): InvShiftRow transformation.

The multiplication in matrix form of S'(r,c)=a(r,c)•S(r,c) which is given in equation (4.10) below can be defined in Equation form as in equations (4.11) to (4.14):-

$$
\begin{pmatrix} S'_{0,c} \\ S'_{1,c} \\ S'_{2,c} \\ S'_{3,c} \end{pmatrix} = \begin{pmatrix} 0e & 0b & 0d & 09 \\ 09 & 0e & 0b & 0d \\ 0d & 09 & 0e & 0b \\ 0b & 0d & 09 & 0e \end{pmatrix} \bullet \begin{pmatrix} S_{0,c} \\ S_{1,c} \\ S_{2,c} \\ S_{3,c} \end{pmatrix} \qquad ....(4.10)
$$

$$S'_{0,c}=(\{0e\}\bullet S_{0,c})\oplus(\{0b\}\bullet S_{1,c})\oplus(\{0d\}\bullet S_{2,c})\oplus(\{09\}\bullet S_{3,c}) \qquad (4.11)$$

$$S'_{1,c}=(\{09\}\bullet S_{0,c})\oplus(\{0e\}\bullet S_{1,c})\oplus(\{0b\}\bullet S_{2,c})\oplus(\{0d\}\bullet S_{3,c}) \qquad (4.12)$$

$$S'_{2,c}=(\{0d\}\bullet S_{0,c})\oplus(\{09\}\bullet S_{1,c})\oplus(\{0e\}\bullet S_{2,c})\oplus(\{0b\}\bullet S_{3,c}) \qquad (4.13)$$

$$S'_{3,c}=(\{0b\}\bullet S_{0,c})\oplus(\{0d\}\bullet S_{1,c})\oplus(\{09\}\bullet S_{2,c})\oplus(\{0e\}\bullet S_{3,c}) \qquad (4.14)$$

From the above equations it can be seen that there are multiplications with 09, 0b, 0d, and 0e. Initially, multiplication with these numbers modulo(x^4+1) in $Gf(2^8)$ is performed as in Figure (4.11).

$$xtime(X_i) = \underline{X}^2{}_i \quad \underline{X}^4{}_i \quad \underline{X}^8{}_i \quad \underline{X}^{10}{}_i \quad \underline{X}^{12}{}_i \text{ - - - - - - - - - - - -}$$

$$X_i \bullet 09 = X_i \oplus X^8{}_i \oplus m(x)$$

$$X_i \bullet 0b = X_i \oplus X^2{}_i \oplus X^8{}_i \oplus m(x)$$

$$X_i \bullet 0d = X_i \oplus X^4{}_i \oplus X^8{}_i \oplus m(x)$$

$$X_i \bullet 0e = X^2{}_i \oplus X^4{}_i \oplus X^8{}_i \oplus m(x)$$

Figure (4.11): Inverse multiplication in $Gf(2^8)$ modulo (x^4+1)

Form the above figure some important facts can be drawn:-

i.   All bytes are multiplied (shifted) according to the xtime function three times.

ii. For each shift of each byte a flag is set if the result is not reduced (an overflow).

iii. At the end of the last shift the three flags for each byte are all XORed. If the result is 1 then the reduction byte would be $m(x) = x^8+x^4+x^3+x+1$ and if the result is 0 then the reduction byte would be $m(x)=0$. The reasons for these decisions are discussed in section (4.5).

iv. Next, it's the XOR operation time where the XORs mentioned in Equations (4.11) through (4.14), the XORs depicted in Figure 4.12 and the XOR with the $m(x)$ are all performed.

The bytes to be multiplied by 0d, and 0e and the reduction byte are XORed. The reduction byte is selected after XORing the six flags of the shift stages of the bytes 0d and 0e. The XOR operation would have seven variables.

The result of this XOR together with the bytes multiplied by 09 and 0b and the reduction byte are XORed and the result would be the InvMixColumned data. The previous description shows the difficulty associated with implementing the InvMixColumn and therefore, the decryption operation.

This stage requires three substages for xtime, and two substages for the XOR operations in addition to the fact that for this design to get its best cost/speed ratio it must be implemented on the virtexII only.

This is also because its XOR operations take seven variables complying with the rule (e) of section (3.7). But the system would stay operating with the same speed and throughput utilized by the encryption implementation.

4.5 The Overall System:

In the previous sections we demonstrated an implementation driven analysis of the encryption algorithm. This along with platform specific parameters helped take the right decisions regarding the target algorithm.

The overall encryption system then comprises (from implementation point of view) two substages for performing the ByteSub transformation, one stage for performing the ShiftRow transformation, two substages for performing the MixColumn transformation and one stage for performing the AddRoundKey operation. This is shown in Figure (4.13).

The controlling criteria in designing the algorithm (and its implementation) in this fashion have been to ensure best speed/cost ratio.

This is combined with the benefits from using piplining approach. Both factors ensure that all stages and substages work synchronously and that these stages give their intended results on the next clock.

For the decryption process, the implementation imposes that the InvByteSub transformation is divided into two sub-stages, the InvShiftRow requires one stage, the InvMixColumn requires five sub-stages and the AddRoundKey requires one stage as shown in Figure (4.14).

The decryption stages in our implementation work with the same clock frequencyof encryption but with more latency time. This is because of the increased number of sub-stages. And this is an expected consequence of piplined architecture.

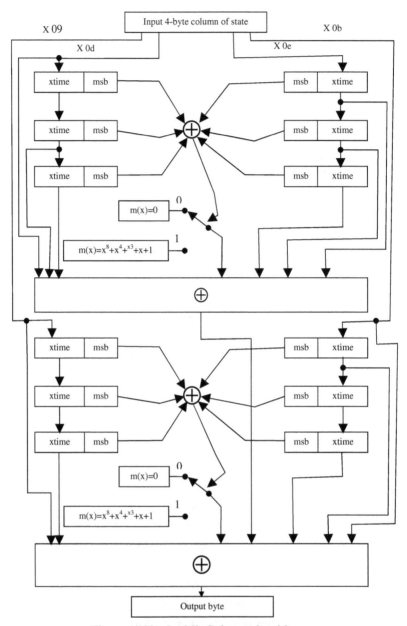

Figure (4.12): InvMixColumn algorithm.

Nonetheless, the increased latency is compensated for by the increased throughput. The evidence for this is that as soon as the pipline gets filled a processed block will be produced at each clock. This is true for encryption as it is for decryption.

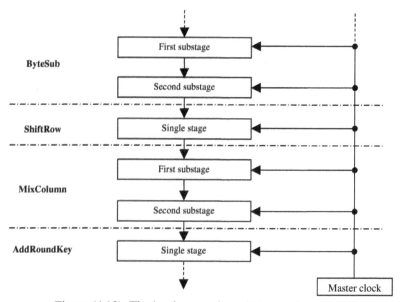

Figure (4.13): The implementation of *i*th round of encryption.

Moreover, having a system with encryption and decryption both working in the same clock frequency is a big deal. It surely gives many benefits, and helps solve many problems especially in connected systems where other algorithms depend on the output of the encryption/decryption algorithm

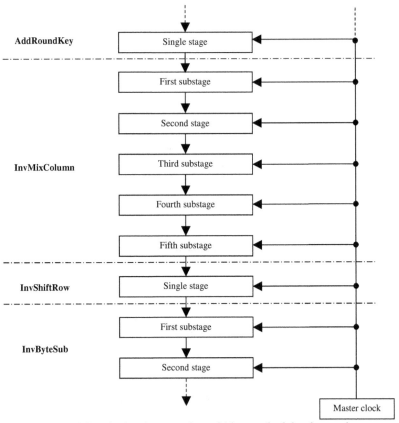

Figure (4.14): The implementation of *i*th round of the decryption.

5

Simulation and Implementation

5.1 Introduction:

The way by which the results can be demonstrated is very important for understanding the effects of any advent or proposition in topic. Figure (5.1) shows the design flow by using VHDL as well as the implementation of the function by using hardware simulators [28].

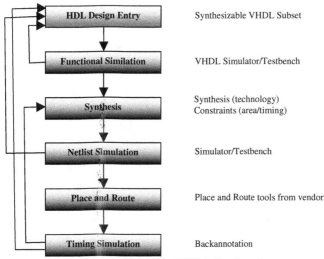

HDL Design Entry	Synthesizable VHDL Subset
Functional Similation	VHDL Simulator/Testbench
Synthesis	Synthesis (technology) Constraints (area/timing)
Netlist Simulation	Simulator/Testbench
Place and Route	Place and Route tools from vendor
Timing Simulation	Backannotation

Figure (5.1): The VHDL Design flow.

This figure emphasizes two main issues to be considered in designing systems with reprogrammable devices; first the fulfillment to operational requirements and second the abidance to the implementation constraints.

Regarding the first issue, there is a needed to assess the ability of the developed VHDL software to produce the kind of output expected from using Rijndael algorithm. This is done by using the ModelSim software tool. We then use the same input used in the example simulated with Matlab® in Chapter 2.

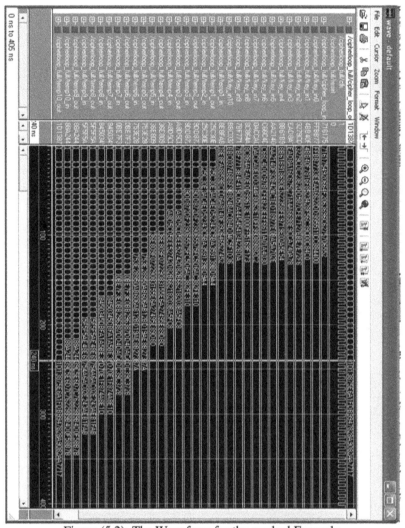

Figure (5.2): The Waveform for the worked Example.

As for the second issue, the VHDL code is submitted to the hardware simulation tool foundation ISE 4.1i. This tool produces several technical reports including the place and route and the timing records.

58

5.2 VHDL Simulation of Rijndael:

As done in the example in Chapter 2, an input text similar to the one used in the worked example is submitted to the VHDL code for comparison of results. The text is converted to the equivalent Hexadecimals. The same key is used for encryption.

After running the simulator we get waveform for the ten rounds of the algorithm as shown in Figure (5.2).

After converting the waveforms into numerical equivalents we get the results shown in Figure (5.3). The results in Figures (5.2) and then (5.3) show that the VHDL code gives the same encryption result as with the Matlab code used in the worked example of Chapter 2.

This means that the proposed VHDL code implements the functionality of the Rijndael algorithm and hence the implementation requirement is fulfilled. What remains then is to show that the proposed implementation outperforms other forms of implementation either completely or partially.

5.3 FPGA Implementation Results:

There are two methods to measure the accuracy of an implemented system: First, by building the system and testing it in offline. This approach is characterized by its high cost, high technical skills while having better accuracy.

The other approach is to use certificated hardware simulation software [12]. In this example we employed the latter approach to reduce cost by employing the Foundation ISE4.1i simulation tool. The outcomes of this approach are a set of reports each of which demonstrates a specific side of the implementation issues.

5.4   Simulation Reports:

There are two simulation groups of reports, namely, the software related and the hardware related reports. Figure (5.4) gives a brief listing of those reports and the category each falls in [12].

Republic Of Iraq

The ASCII equivalents of the statement (in Hex.):

52 62 20 49

65 6c 4f 75

70 69 66 61

75 63 20 71

The initial key (in Hex):

00 44 88 cc

11 55 99 dd

22 66 aa ee

33 77 bb ff

The output Cipher (in Hex):

17 90 99 5e

77 8a db 87

aa 82 1f 13

82 47 6a 1d

Figure (5.3) The Equivalent data.

5.4.1 *The Content of the Software Reports:*

There are two reports that include all the necessary information about the simulation programs that are used in the implementation of the design in the final step of the program:

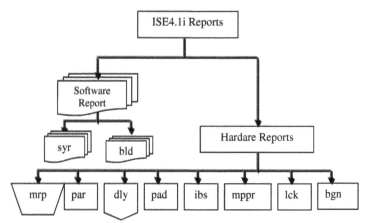

Figure (5.4): Classification of ISE4.1i reports.

First: the *view synthesis* report is given the symbol **syr**. This report is the general description of the options of the program which has the following parameters:

a) The source parameters that cover the type of language as well as the name of program.
b) Target parameters which give the type of chip, output file name, output format and the target technology.
c) Source options that have the following items:
   i. Entity name.
   ii. Finite State Machine (FSM) extraction.
   iii. FSM encoding algorithm.
   iv. FSM flip-flop type.
   v. MUX extraction.
   vi. Resource sharing.
   vii. Complex clocks enable extraction.
   viii. Multiplier style.
   ix. ROM extraction.
   x. RAM extraction.
   xi. RAM style.
   xii. MUX style.
   xiii. Decoder extraction.
   xiv. Priority encoder extraction.

xv.   Shift registers extraction.

xvi.   Logical shifter extraction.

xvii.   XOR collapsing.

xviii. Register balancing.

   d) Target options that have the following items:

   i.   Additional IO buffers.

   ii.   Equivalent register removal.

   iii.   Additional generic clock buffer (BUFG).

   iv.   Global maximum fanout.

   v.   Register duplication.

   vi.   Move first flipflop stage.

   vii.   Move last flipflop stage

   viii.   Slice packing

   ix.   Pack IO registers into IOBs

   x.   Speed grade.

Second: the ***translation*** report that is named **bld** which contains the warning and error messages of the three translation processes. These processes are the conversion of the EDIF netlist to the Xilinx NGD netlist format, the timing specification checks and the logical design rule checks. The report lists the followings:

   a) Missing or untranslatable hierarchical blocks.

   b) Invalid or incomplete timing constraints and removed logic summary.

   c) Output contention, loadless outputs and sourceless inputs.

5.4.2 The Content of the Hardware Reports:

The hardware reports describe the second step of the design required to give a complete view of the implemented system. These are eight reports as shown in Figure (5.4). It's important to mention that the **mrp** and **dly** reports are the most important of these reports.

a) The *map desecration* report named **mrp** contains the warning and error messages detailing logic optimization and problems in mapping logic to physical resources. The report lists the following information:

i.	Errors
ii.	Warnings
iii.	Informational
iv.	Removed Logic Summary
v.	Removed Logic
vi.	IOB Properties
vii.	RPMs
viii.	Guide Report
ix.	Area Group Summary
x.	Modular Design Summary

b) The second hardware report is the *place and route* report that is named **par**. This report contains the following information:

i.   The number of external IOBs.

ii.   The number of LOCed (not connected in the internally circuit) external IOBs.

iii.   The number of slices that are required to implement the design.

iv.   The overall placer score which measures the "goodness" of the placement. The goodness score depends on the number of internal intersection nodes. Note that, the lower score gives better results. The number of signals not completely routed should be zero for a steady state completely implemented design. If it is a non-zero, the designer may be able to improve the results by using re-entrant routing or the multi-pass place and route flow.

v.   The timing summary at the end of the report details the design's asynchronous delays.

c) The *asynchronous delay* report that is named **dly** is the most important one which consists of about 6000 pages that list all nets in the design and the delays of all loads on the net. The 20th highest net delays are listed at the top of the report.

d) The *pad* report lists the design's pinout in three ways. Signals are referenced according to pad numbers. The pad numbers are referenced according to signal names.

e) The *IBIS model* for Virtex-II report is named **ibs.** This report is the general description for the chip pins of the IC that is used in the implementation of the system with full description of all its pins. This report has in each pin the following points:

   i.   The function of the input/output pins and their connections.
   ii.   The delay to input or output data in each pin.
   iii. All the currents in the main connections of each I/O pin with typically, the maximum and the minimum estimated current.
   iv. All the voltages of the point of the I/O port in each connection.
   v.   The input resistance value.
   vi. The input capacitor value.

f) The generator of the *multi-pass place and route* report named **MPPR** lists the design scores and timing scores for the design after checking all the hardware reports for error or missing in them.

g) The *back-annotate pin* report that is named **lck** provides the information on the constraint conflicts if the pin of units and connections file (ucf) is found. The ucf uses the provided design and those existing in the design after the generation of the **MPPR** report.

There are two types of conflicts that may occur:

   i.   Multiple pins could be constrained on the same net.
   ii.   The same pin could have multiple nets.

h) The last report is the *programming file generating* report that is named **bgn.** This report has the summary of bit generation options for the loading chip. This report will be used in the last step in the implantation of the system.

5.5 Summary of Reports for *Virtex-E:*

a) The Map Report Rijndael algorithm:- Design Summary

Number of Slices:	2,304
Number of Slice Flip Flops:	10,448
Number of bonded IOBs:	129
Total equivalent gate count for design:	27,460

b) The Asynchronous Delay Report of Rijndael algorithm:-

We have attempted to summarize this report in two main data pieces making use of the most critical indicators in this report these are:

i.   The simulated maximum operational frequency is 141MHz.

ii. The maximum asynchronous delay time is 7.08 ns

5.6 Summary of Reports for Virtex-II:

a) The Map Report of Rijndael algorithm: Design Summary

Number of Slices:	2,658 out of 61,440	4%
Number of Slice Flip Flops:	2,486 out of 122,880	2%
Number 4 input LUTs:	3,598 out of 122,880	2%
Number of bonded IOBs:	129 out of 1,108	11%
Total equivalent gate count for design:	48,949	

b) The Asynchronous Delay Report of Rijndael algorithm:-

i.   The simulated maximum operational frequency is 182MHz.

ii. The maximum asynchronous delay time is 5.497 ns.

The timing reports for this design are included in Appendix C.

5.7 Compared Results:

The proposed design gives high record parameters compared to other implementations. Those implementation were discussed briefly in the Chapter 1. These designs are optimized for speed. The comparison results are given in Table (5.1) and Table (5.2).

The parameters used for qualification are the number of slices. This shows the cost of implementation; The operational frequency which shows the maximum speed for purposes of synchronization with other systems (interoperability).The throughput of the system which shows how much data could be processed per unit time and finally the throughput per Slice (TPS) which is a combination measure that shows how optimal the design is in terms of cost and speed (volume of data).

Hence, TPS = throughput of the design / number of slices used.

Table 5.1: A comparison of proposed design (VirtexII) with other designs

	Prop. VirtexII	Weaver Virex-E [5]	Weaver Spartan [11]	Amphion [6]	Chodowiec 1 [7]	Kown [8]	Chodowiec 2 [7]	Elbirit [9]
# Slice	2658	770	770	570	222	2256	1228	4871
f_{max} (MHz)	182	155	115	/	50	30	47	/
Throughput (Gb/s)	23.296	1.75	1.3	1.06	0.147	0.167	0.521	1.94
TPS (Mb/s)	8.76	2.3	1.7	1.9	0.63	0.074	0.424	0.195

Table 5.2: A comparison of proposed design (VirtexE) with other designs

	Prop. Virtex E	Weaver Virex-E [5]	Weaver Spartan [11]	Amphion [6]	Chodowiec 1 [7]	Kown [8]	Chodowiec 2 [7]	Elbirit [9]
# Slice	2304	770	770	570	222	2256	1228	4871
f_{max} (MHz)	141	155	115	/	50	30	47	/
Throughput (Gb/s)	18.048	1.75	1.3	1.06	0.147	0.167	0.521	1.94
TPS (Mb/s)	7.833	2.3	1.7	1.9	0.63	0.074	0.424	0.195

Appendix A

The detailed encryption process for the worked example of Chapter 2:

Initial matrix State:

52 62 20 49
65 6c 4f 75
70 69 66 61
75 63 20 71

Initial round key :

00 44 88 cc
11 55 99 dd
22 66 aa ee
33 77 bb ff

State at start of round 1 :

52 26 a8 85
74 39 d6 a8
52 0f cc 8f
46 14 9b 8e

After sub_bytes :

00 f7 c2 97
92 12 f6 c2
00 76 4b 73
5a fa 14 19

After shift_rows :

00 f7 c2 97
12 f6 c2 92
4b 73 00 76
19 5a fa 14

After mix_columns :

64 dd 38 fa

e0 cf a7 26
af 09 15 d5
6b 33 70 6e

Round key :

c0 84 0c c0
39 6c f5 28
34 52 f8 16
78 0f b4 4b

State at start of round 2 :

a4 59 34 3a
d9 a3 52 0e
9b 5b ed c3
13 3c c4 25

After sub_bytes :

49 cb 18 80
35 0a 00 ab
14 39 55 2e
7d eb 1c 3f

After shift_rows :

49 cb 18 80
0a 00 ab 35
55 2e 14 39
3f 7d eb 1c

After mix_columns :

e6 de 29 61
9d c4 82 bd
a8 10 bd e3
fa 92 5a af

Round key :

f6 72 7e be
7e 12 e7 cf
87 d5 2d 3b
c2 cd 79 32

State at start of round 3 :
10 ac 57 df
e3 d6 65 72
2f c5 90 d8
38 5f 23 9d

After sub_bytes :
ca 91 5b 9e
11 f6 4d 40
15 a6 60 61
07 cf 26 5e

After shift_rows :
ca 91 5b 9e
f6 4d 40 11
60 61 15 a6
5e 07 cf 26

After mix_columns :
b0 88 ac 94
c3 af 2b 6b
1e 17 7b b2
6f 8a 3d 42

Round key :
78 0a 74 ca
9c 8e 69 a6
a4 71 5c 67
6c a1 d8 ea

State at start of round 4 :

        c8 82 d8 5e
        5f 21 42 cd
        ba 66 27 d5
        03 2b e5 a8

After sub_bytes :

        e8 13 61 58
        cf fd 2c bd
        f4 33 cc 03
        7b f1 d9 c2

After shift_rows :

        e8 13 61 58
        fd 2c bd cf
        cc 03 f4 33
        c2 7b f1 d9

After mix_columns :

        d9 2a 1b 10
        84 35 f6 51
        cb b4 27 81
        8d ec 13 bd

Round key :

        54 5e 2a e0
        19 97 fe 58
        23 52 0e 69
        18 b9 61 8b

State at start of round 5 :

        8d 74 31 f0
        9d a2 08 09
        e8 e6 29 e8
        95 55 72 36

After sub_bytes :

5d 92 c7 8c
5e 3a 30 01
9b 8e a5 9b
2a fc 40 05

After shift_rows :

5d 92 c7 8c
3a 30 01 5e
a5 9b 9b 8e
05 2a fc 40

After mix_columns :

54 de f1 2f
d8 6e 8f f9
39 f1 f4 15
72 52 2b df

Round key :

2e 70 5a ba
e0 77 89 d1
1e 4c 42 2b
f9 40 21 aa

State at start of round 6 :

7a ae ab 95
38 19 06 28
27 bd b6 3e
8b 12 0a 75

After sub_bytes :

da e4 62 2a
07 d4 6f 34
cc 7a 4e b2

                     3d c9 67 9d

After shift_rows :

                     da e4 62 2a
                     d4 6f 34 07
                     4e b2 cc 7a
                     9d 3d c9 67

After mix_columns :

                     1b ed 9d 40
                     26 ca 8c cd
                     2e b3 95 70
                     ce 90 d7 cd

Round key :

                     30 40 1a a0
                     11 66 ef 3e
                     b2 fe bc 97
                     0d 4d 6c c6

State at start of round 7 :

                     2b ad 87 e0
                     37 ac 63 f3
                     9c 4d 29 e7
                     c3 dd bb 0b

After sub_bytes :

                     f1 95 17 e1
                     9a 91 fb 0d
                     de e3 a5 94
                     2e c1 ea 2b

After shift_rows :

                     f1 95 17 e1
                     91 fb 0d 9a

a5 94 de e3

2b 2e c1 ea

After mix_columns :

df 9d 26 65

17 f1 b5 1a

4c 2f e5 83

6a 97 73 8e

Round key :

c2 82 98 38

99 ff 10 2e

06 f8 44 d3

ed a0 cc 0a

State at start of round 8 :

1d 1f be 5d

8e 0e a5 34

4a d7 a1 50

87 37 bf 84

After sub_bytes :

a4 c0 ae 4c

19 ab 06 18

d6 0e 32 53

17 9a 08 5f

After shift_rows :

a4 c0 ae 4c

ab 06 18 19

32 53 d6 0e

5f 17 9a 08

After mix_columns :

d8 d5 23 b5

e0 2e 65 64
8a 59 b4 51
d0 20 08 d3

Round key :

73 f1 69 51
ff 00 10 3e
61 99 dd 0e
ea 4a 86 8c

State at start of round 9 :

ab 24 4a e4
1f 2e 75 5a
eb c0 69 5f
3a 6a 8e 5f

After sub_bytes :

62 36 d6 69
c0 31 9d be
e9 ba f9 cf
80 02 19 cf

After shift_rows :

62 36 d6 69
31 9d be c0
f9 cf e9 ba
cf 80 02 19

After mix_columns :

a1 9f 85 2a
df dd 93 3e
f0 b5 a7 ed
eb 13 32 f3

Round key :

da 2b 42 13
54 54 44 7a
05 9c 41 4f
3b 71 f7 7b

State at start of final round :

7b b4 c7 39
8b 89 d7 44
f5 29 e6 a2
d0 62 c5 88

After sub_bytes :

21 8d c6 12
3d a7 0e 1b
e6 a5 8e 3a
70 aa a6 c4

After shift_rows :

21 8d c6 12
a7 0e 1b 3d
8e 3a e6 a5
c4 70 aa a6

Round key :

36 1d 5f 4c
d0 84 c0 ba
24 b8 f9 b6
46 37 c0 bb

Final state :

17 90 99 5e
77 8a db 87
aa 82 1f 13
82 47 6a 1d

Appendix B

B.1 Multiplication in Gf(2^8)[16]:

In polynomial representation multiplication in Gf(2^8) (denoted by •) corresponds to the multiplication of polynomials modulo an irreducible polynomial of degree 8.

A polynomial is irreducible if its only divisors are one and itself. For the Rijndael algorithm this irreducible polynomial is given below:

$$m(x) = x^8 + x^4 + x^3 + x + 1,$$ B.1

or, {01}{1b} in hexadecimal notation.

For example, {57}•{83} = {c1} because:

$$(x^6 + x^4 + x^2 + x + 1)(x^7 + x + 1) = x^{13} + x^{11} + x^9 + x^8 + x^7 + x^7 + x^5 + x^3 + x^2$$
$$+ x + x^6 + x^4 + x^2 + x + 1$$
$$= x^{13} + x^{11} + x^9 + x^8 + x^6 + x^5 + x^4 + x^3 + 1$$

and

$$x^{13} + x^{11} + x^9 + x^8 + x^6 + x^5 + x^4 + x^3 + 1 \text{ modulo } (x^8 + x^4 + x^3 + x + 1)$$
$$= x^7 + x^6 + 1.$$

The modular reduction by $m(x)$ ensures that the result will be a binary polynomial of degree less than 8 and thus, it can be represented by a byte. The multiplication defined above is associative and the element {01} is the multiplicative identity.

For any non-zero binary polynomial $b(x)$ of degree less than 8, the multiplicative inverse of $b(x)$ denoted $b^{-1}(x)$ can be found as follows:

The extended Euclidean algorithm [21] is used to compute polynomials $a(c)$ such that:

$$b(x) \bullet a(x) + m(x)c(x) = 1$$ B.2

Hence, $a(x)•b(x) \bmod m(x) = 1$, which means:
$$b^{-1}(x) = a(x) \bmod m(x)$$ B.3

Moreover, for any $a(x)$, $b(x)$ and $c(x)$ in the field, it holds that:

$$a(x)\bullet(b(x) + c(x)) = a(x)\bullet b(x) + a(x)\bullet c(x).$$

It follows that the set of 256 possible byte values with XOR used as addition and the multiplication defined as above has the structure of the finite field $Gf(2^8)$.

B.2 Multiplication by x and the xtime Function [11]:

Multiplying the following binary polynomial defined in equation B.4 with the polynomial x results in equation B.5

$$b_7x^7 + b_6x^6 + b_5x^5 + b_4x^4 + b_3x^3 + b_2x^2 + b_1x + b_0 = \sum_{i=0}^{7} b_i\, x^i \qquad \text{(B.4)}$$

$$b_7x^8 + b_6x^7 + b_5x^6 + b_4x^5 + b_3x^4 + b_2x^3 + b_1x^2 + b_0\, x \qquad \text{(B.5)}$$

The result $x\bullet b(x)$ is obtained by reducing the above result modulo $m(x)$ as defined in equation (B.1). If $b_7=0$ the result is already in reduced form. If $b_7=1$ then the reduction is accomplished by subtracting (i.e., XORing) the polynomial $m(x)$. It follows that multiplication by x (i.e., 00000010 or {02}) can be implemented at the byte level as a left shift and a subsequent conditional bitwise XOR with {1b}.

This operation on bytes is denoted by xtime(). Multiplication by higher powers can be implemented by repeated application of xtime(). By adding intermediate results multiplication by any constant can be implemented.

For example, {57}•{13} = {fe} as follows:

$$\{57\}\bullet\{02\} = \text{xtime}(\{57\}) = \{ae\}$$
$$\{57\}\bullet\{04\} = \text{xtime}(\{ae\}) = \{47\}$$
$$\{57\}\bullet\{08\} = \text{xtime}(\{47\}) = \{8e\}$$
$$\{57\}\bullet\{10\} = \text{xtime}(\{8e\}) = \{07\},$$

Thus,

$$\{57\} \cdot \{13\} = \{57\} \cdot (\{01\} \oplus \{02\} \oplus \{10\})$$
$$= \{57\} \oplus \{ae\} \oplus \{07\}$$
$$= \{fe\}.$$

Appendix C
Timing Reports

Release 4.1i - Trace E.30
Copyright (c) 1995-2001 Xilinx, Inc. All rights reserved.

trce -e 3 -l 3 -xml cipherloop_full cipherloop_full.ncd -o cipherloop_full.twr
cipherloop_full.pcf

Design file: *cipherloop_full.ncd*
Physical constraint file: cipherloop_full.pcf
Device,speed: *xc2v10000,-5 (ADVANCED 1.85 2001-07-24)*
Report level: *error report*

WARNING:Timing - No timing constraints found, doing default enumeration.

==
====
Timing constraint: Default period analysis

 19097 items analyzed, 0 timing errors detected.
 Minimum period is   4.668ns.
 Maximum delay is 11.394ns.

==
====
Timing constraint: Default net enumeration

 5456 items analyzed, 0 timing errors detected.
 Maximum net delay is   5.497ns.

All constraints were met.

Data Sheet report:

All values displayed in nanoseconds (ns)
Clock clk to Pad
-------------------+------------+
         | clk (edge) |

81

Destination Pad	to PAD
cipher_loop_out<0>	13.982(R)
cipher_loop_out<100>	16.050(R)
cipher_loop_out<101>	15.709(R)
cipher_loop_out<102>	16.022(R)
cipher_loop_out<103>	15.892(R)
cipher_loop_out<104>	13.780(R)
cipher_loop_out<105>	14.936(R)
cipher_loop_out<106>	14.059(R)
cipher_loop_out<107>	15.253(R)
cipher_loop_out<108>	15.030(R)
cipher_loop_out<109>	15.006(R)
cipher_loop_out<10>	14.781(R)
cipher_loop_out<110>	13.912(R)
cipher_loop_out<111>	15.103(R)
cipher_loop_out<112>	15.286(R)
cipher_loop_out<113>	13.922(R)
cipher_loop_out<114>	13.931(R)
cipher_loop_out<115>	15.161(R)
cipher_loop_out<116>	13.944(R)
cipher_loop_out<117>	15.338(R)
cipher_loop_out<118>	14.858(R)
cipher_loop_out<119>	14.961(R)
cipher_loop_out<11>	14.679(R)
cipher_loop_out<120>	14.121(R)
cipher_loop_out<121>	14.028(R)
cipher_loop_out<122>	13.663(R)
cipher_loop_out<123>	15.076(R)
cipher_loop_out<124>	15.048(R)
cipher_loop_out<125>	15.036(R)
cipher_loop_out<126>	15.383(R)
cipher_loop_out<127>	14.955(R)
cipher_loop_out<12>	15.117(R)
cipher_loop_out<13>	14.894(R)
cipher_loop_out<14>	14.783(R)
cipher_loop_out<15>	14.635(R)
cipher_loop_out<16>	16.756(R)
cipher_loop_out<17>	14.113(R)
cipher_loop_out<18>	13.680(R)
cipher_loop_out<19>	13.817(R)
cipher_loop_out<1>	13.878(R)
cipher_loop_out<20>	15.287(R)
cipher_loop_out<21>	15.132(R)

cipher_loop_out<22>	*14.622(R)*	
cipher_loop_out<23>	*14.776(R)*	
cipher_loop_out<24>	*13.874(R)*	
cipher_loop_out<25>	*16.208(R)*	
cipher_loop_out<26>	*14.152(R)*	
cipher_loop_out<27>	*14.613(R)*	
cipher_loop_out<28>	*13.674(R)*	
cipher_loop_out<29>	*13.703(R)*	
cipher_loop_out<2>	*13.615(R)*	
cipher_loop_out<30>	*14.299(R)*	
cipher_loop_out<31>	*15.027(R)*	
cipher_loop_out<32>	*15.823(R)*	
cipher_loop_out<33>	*14.225(R)*	
cipher_loop_out<34>	*15.763(R)*	
cipher_loop_out<35>	*14.425(R)*	
cipher_loop_out<36>	*14.030(R)*	
cipher_loop_out<37>	*13.995(R)*	
cipher_loop_out<38>	*13.985(R)*	
cipher_loop_out<39>	*13.518(R)*	
cipher_loop_out<3>	*13.812(R)*	
cipher_loop_out<40>	*16.522(R)*	
cipher_loop_out<41>	*13.540(R)*	
cipher_loop_out<42>	*13.772(R)*	
cipher_loop_out<43>	*13.919(R)*	
cipher_loop_out<44>	*13.772(R)*	
cipher_loop_out<45>	*13.939(R)*	
cipher_loop_out<46>	*13.982(R)*	
cipher_loop_out<47>	*14.024(R)*	
cipher_loop_out<48>	*16.066(R)*	
cipher_loop_out<49>	*13.743(R)*	
cipher_loop_out<4>	*13.462(R)*	
cipher_loop_out<50>	*14.587(R)*	
cipher_loop_out<51>	*13.830(R)*	
cipher_loop_out<52>	*14.002(R)*	
cipher_loop_out<53>	*13.507(R)*	
cipher_loop_out<54>	*13.400(R)*	
cipher_loop_out<55>	*13.753(R)*	
cipher_loop_out<56>	*13.898(R)*	
cipher_loop_out<57>	*15.008(R)*	
cipher_loop_out<58>	*15.142(R)*	
cipher_loop_out<59>	*14.805(R)*	
cipher_loop_out<5>	*13.659(R)*	
cipher_loop_out<60>	*13.546(R)*	
cipher_loop_out<61>	*14.663(R)*	

```
cipher_loop_out<62>  |  13.956(R)|
cipher_loop_out<63>  |  14.267(R)|
cipher_loop_out<64>  |  15.443(R)|
cipher_loop_out<65>  |  14.070(R)|
cipher_loop_out<66>  |  15.809(R)|
cipher_loop_out<67>  |  13.763(R)|
cipher_loop_out<68>  |  15.970(R)|
cipher_loop_out<69>  |  13.532(R)|
cipher_loop_out<6>   |  13.985(R)|
cipher_loop_out<70>  |  14.420(R)|
cipher_loop_out<71>  |  15.499(R)|
cipher_loop_out<72>  |  13.335(R)|
cipher_loop_out<73>  |  13.856(R)|
cipher_loop_out<74>  |  13.463(R)|
cipher_loop_out<75>  |  15.402(R)|
cipher_loop_out<76>  |  15.159(R)|
cipher_loop_out<77>  |  14.052(R)|
cipher_loop_out<78>  |  13.790(R)|
cipher_loop_out<79>  |  15.538(R)|
cipher_loop_out<7>   |  13.684(R)|
cipher_loop_out<80>  |  13.838(R)|
cipher_loop_out<81>  |  14.084(R)|
cipher_loop_out<82>  |  14.455(R)|
cipher_loop_out<83>  |  14.090(R)|
cipher_loop_out<84>  |  15.224(R)|
cipher_loop_out<85>  |  14.243(R)|
cipher_loop_out<86>  |  14.952(R)|
cipher_loop_out<87>  |  14.946(R)|
cipher_loop_out<88>  |  14.755(R)|
cipher_loop_out<89>  |  13.757(R)|
cipher_loop_out<8>   |  15.149(R)|
cipher_loop_out<90>  |  14.192(R)|
cipher_loop_out<91>  |  14.466(R)|
cipher_loop_out<92>  |  14.805(R)|
cipher_loop_out<93>  |  16.803(R)|
cipher_loop_out<94>  |  14.379(R)|
cipher_loop_out<95>  |  15.389(R)|
cipher_loop_out<96>  |  13.431(R)|
cipher_loop_out<97>  |  13.458(R)|
cipher_loop_out<98>  |  15.130(R)|
cipher_loop_out<99>  |  13.817(R)|
cipher_loop_out<9>   |  13.923(R)|
--------------------------+------------+
```

Clock to Setup on destination clock clk
```
-----------+----------+----------+----------+----------+
          | Src:Rise| Src:Fall| Src:Rise| Src:Fall|
Source Clock  |Dest:Rise|Dest:Rise|Dest:Fall|Dest:Fall|
------------------+-----------+-----------+-----------+----------+
clk        |   4.668|      |     |      |
-----------+---------+------+-----+------+
```

Timing summary:
```
---------------
```

Timing errors: 0 Score: 0

Constraints cover 19097 paths, 5456 nets, and 21318 connections (100.0% coverage)

Analysis completed Sun Jul 10 01:42:49 2005
```
--------------------------------------------------------------------------------
```
Timing Reports

References:

[1]   William Stallings, "Cryptography and Network Security: Principles and Practice", Prentice Hall 2003.

[2]   A. Menezes, P. van, "Handbook of Applied Cryptography" Oorschot, and S. Vanstone, CRC Press, 1996.

[3]   CHEUNG Yu Hoi Ocean (B. Eng.),"Implementation of an FPGA Based Accelerator for Virtual Private Networks", Computer Science and Engineering, The Chinese University of Hong Kong, 10th July, 2002

[4]   Nicolas Weaver and John Wawrznynek "Spartan Throughput", 2004, www.cs.berkely.edu/~nweaver/rijndael.

[5]   Nicolas Weaver and John Wawrznynek, "High Performance, Compact AES Implementation in Xilinx FPGAs Virtex E", 2004.

[6]   Amphion Semiconductor, "High Performance AES Encryption Cores", www.amphion.com/cs5210.html, 2003.

[7]   Pawel Chodowiec, and Kris Gaj, "Very Compact FPGA Implementation of the AES Algorithm", International Symposium on FPGA, 2003

[8]   Ohjun Kwon et al, "Implementation of AES and Triple DES Cryptography Using a PCI-based FPGA Board", National Defence Academy, 2002.

[9]   AJ Elbirt, W Yip, B Chetwynd and C Paar, "An FPGA-Based Performance Evaluation of the AES Block Cipher Candidate Algorithm Finalists", ECE Department, Worcester Polytechnic Institute, 2002.

[10]   Siddeeq Y Ameen, "Security Srvices Provision and Enhancement in Client/Server Networks using AES", Journal of computer and communication and control engineering, Department of Computer Engineering and Information Technology, University of Technology, 2005.

[11]   Bruce Schneier, "Applied Cryptography", 2ed .New York .John Willey, 1996.

[12]   Michael Welschenbach, "Cryptography in C and C++", APress, 2001.

[13]   John E. Canavan, "Fundamentals of Network Security", Artech House, Boston, http://www.artechhouse.com, 2001.

[14]   Federal Information Processing Standards Publication 197, Announcing The Advanced Encryption Standard AES, November 26, 2001.

[15]   NIST, "Commerce Department Announcing Rijndael as the New AES", www.nist.gov/public_affairs/releases/g00-176.html . Aug 25, 2001.

[16]   J. Daemen and V. Rijmen, "The Block Cipher Rijndael", http://www.nist.gov/aes, 2001.

[17]   Atiniramit, P, "Design and Implementation of an FPGA-based Adaptive filter Single-User Receiver", Blacksburg, Virginia, September 17, 1999.

[18]   Dhafer R. Zaghar, "Design and Implementation of General Digital Down Converter Using Field Programable Gate Array", PhD Thesis, electrical engineering, college of engineering of university of Baghdad, 2002.

[19]   Dueck, "Digital Design with CPLD Applications and VHDL", Dec. 2001.

[20]   Mano and Kime, "Programmable Logic ROM, PAL, CPLD, FPGA", Programmable, 378, 1998.

[21]   S Brown and J Rose, "Architecture of FPGAs and CPLDs: A Tutorial", , Department of Electrical and Computer Engineering, University of Toronto, 2003.

[22]   Carmichael, C., "Configuring Virtex FPGAs from Parallel EPROMs with a CPLD", Application Note, XAPP 137, Version 1.0. March 1, 1999.

[23]   M Alwan, "Design of Field Programmable Gate Array Based Digital Filters", Basrah university, Ph.D. Thesis, 2002.

[24]   Altera_flex, "Altera FLEX methodology - Details ", http://www./altera_flex_meth.htm, 2004.

[25]   Advance Product Specification, "XC17V00 Series Configuration PROM", DS073 (v1.5) October 9, 2001.

[26]   Advance Product Specification, "Virtex-E 1.8 V Field Programmable Gate Arrays", DS022 (v1.0) December 7, 1999.

[27]   Xilinx, "DSP Implementation Techniques for Xilinx FPGAs", http://support.xilinx.com/support/training/training.htm, 2004.

[28]   K Goldblatt, "The Express Configuration of Spartan-XL FPGAs", Application Note Version 1.0, XAPP 122 Nov 13, 1998.

[29]   S Brown and Z Vranesic, "Fundamental of Digital Logic with VHDL Design", McGraw-Hill, 2000.

[30]   R. L Walke and R. Smith, "Architectures for Adaptive Weight Calculation on ASIC and FPGA", DERA (Malvern), St. Andrews Road, Malvern, WR14 3PS, UK, 2003.

[31]   S Yalamanchili, "Introductory VHDL: From Simulation To Synthesis", Prentice Hall Xilinx Design Series, Prentice Hall, 2001.

[32]   Graphics, M., "ModelSim SE/EE PLUS 5.4a", Model Technology Incorporated, http://www.model.com, Apr. 2000.

[33]   J. Bhasker, "VHDL Primer", 3rd edition, Bell laboratories, Lucent technologies, Allenton, PA, Prentice Hall, 1999.

[34]   "VHDL Design Methodology Syntax and Commands", VHDL fÜr XILINX Folie 1 von 478, 2003.